JOHN DEWEY

JOHN DEWEY

AN INTELLECTUAL PORTRAIT

BY
SIDNEY HOOK

INTRODUCTION BY
RICHARD RORTY

Prometheus Books

59 John Glenn Drive
Amherst, New York 14228-2197

Published 1995 by Prometheus Books
in cooperation with The John Dewey Foundation,
Suite 1007, 570 Seventh Avenue, New York, NY 10018

99 98 97 96 95   5 4 3 2 1

Library of Congress Cataloging-in-Publication Data

Hook, Sidney, 1902–1991
    John Dewey : an intellectual portrait / by Sidney Hook ; with
an introduction by Richard Rorty.
        p.   cm.
    Originally published: 1939.
    Includes bibliographical references.
    ISBN 0-87975-985-2 (hc : alk. paper)
    1. Dewey, John, 1859–1952. I. Title.
B945.D44H47   1995
191—dc20   95-2887
                                                              CIP

Printed in the United States of America on acid-free paper.

TO JOHNNIE

TO HELP HIM GROW

CONTENTS

PREFACE

This year John Dewey enters upon the ninth decade of his life. Instead of offering a biography of a man who is still very much in the thick of things, I have attempted a study of the leading ideas of his philosophy. My hope is, by a clear and nontechnical statement of his central insights and their implications, to give to the intelligent layman and the beginning student of philosophy a sense of the sweep and vitality of John Dewey's vision, as well as an understanding of the relevance of his contributions to the problems of American culture.

In expounding the ideas of a man whose writings span a period of more than half a century, an element of emphasis and selection is unavoidable. In this sense my exposition is also an interpretation. Its fidelity can be verified only by a first-hand experience with Dewey's own writings. There is some pedagogical evidence that Dewey's most important doctrines are not easy to grasp, even by those of his popular critics who have followed the unusual course of reading him. What I have attempted to do in this intellectual portrait is to furnish an introduction to Dewey's philosophy in which particular attention is paid to the kind of difficulties likely to arise in the minds of readers. It is therefore not out of conventional modesty that I am led to say that my chief purpose will have been served if the reader is moved by this enterprise to make a study and independent evaluation of John Dewey's own writings.

Sidney Hook

South Wardsboro, Vermont
September 1, 1939

INTRODUCTION

Nostalgia is unbecoming to pragmatists, who are supposed to look forward rather than back. Nonetheless, it is hard to reread either John Dewey or Sidney Hook without feeling that there were giants in those days. The scope of both men's reading and writing, as well as the sheer vitality of their minds, are hard to match among present-day American philosophers—or, for that matter, American intellectuals. Both men resemble such heroic nineteenth-century figures as John Stuart Mill in the sheer quantity of work they managed to get done, in the range of their curiosity, and in their ability to switch back and forth between abstract philosophy and concrete social issues with no sense of strain and no diminution in intensity.

Hook's 1939 book on Dewey remains the best short introduction to the latter's thought.[1] Fifty-six years after publication, its only drawbacks are those that Hook himself would have predicted. It was written with an eye to the philosophical and political scene of the 1930s, and things have changed. Logical

---

1. Those who wish to consult more recent treatments of Dewey should look at three books that testify to a recent rebirth of interest in his thought and influence: Robert Westbrook's magisterial intellectual biography *John Dewey and American Democracy* (1991); Steven Rockefeller's *John Dewey: Religious Faith and Democratic Humanism* (1991); Alan Ryan's *John Dewey and the High Tide of American Liberalism* (1995).

empiricism (the thirties' and forties' version of what is now called "analytic philosophy") is no longer taken very seriously. Neither is Marxism. Hook had, as this book shows, immersed himself in both movements.

By 1939 Hook was convinced that pragmatism and social democratic politics could do everything that Marxism could do. He had put Marx and Marxism, on both of which he had written brilliantly, behind him. But he saw logical empiricism—the movement represented by Russell, Carnap, and Ayer—as promising and as having a lot in common with Deweyan pragmatism. Like his friend Ernest Nagel, he hoped that a shared respect for natural science might permit some sort of alliance between the two philosophical movements. But he thought that the logical empiricists needed to get rid of the idea of "sense data." Further, he agreed, as did Dewey, with many of Hegel's criticisms of Kant and thought of Fregeans like Carnap as still too much under Kant's spell.

In the last fifty years, the analytic philosophers (who make up the vast majority of teachers of philosophy in the English-speaking world) have repudiated most of the Kantian notions to which Hook and Dewey objected.[2] They no longer talk much about "sensory givenness," nor about "conceptual truths." But they have also remained rather suspicious of Dewey and of pragmatism—and, even more, of Hegel. One reason for this is that Dewey's conception of philosophy as social criticism is remote from theirs. The hyperprofessional-

2. See Morton White's *Toward Reunion in Philosophy* (1956) for what is still the best account of the gradual reconciliation of Deweyan naturalism with logical empiricism, a reconciliation facilitated by Quine's criticism of the analytic-synthetic distinction and by Wittgenstein's scorn for his earlier conviction that logic is "something sublime."

ism that has become characteristic of analytic philosophy has created a philosophical climate very different from the one that Dewey and Hook hoped to bring about.

Kant is the archetypal philosophical professional—the man who established philosophy as an autonomous academic discipline. In contrast, Hegel's and Marx's willingness to think of everything as up for historical grabs makes them inappropriate models for philosophy professors who think of "enduring problems" as their primary topics. Dewey and Hook, by contrast, thought that, even though Hegel and Marx had bitten off more than they could chew, these two critics of Kant had had the right idea about what philosophers should do. Philosophers should try, as Hegel put it, to hold their time in thought. Dewey hoped that his colleagues would come to agree that "the task of future philosophy is to clarify men's ideas as to the social and moral strifes of their own day."[3]

Some philosophers of our own day—notably Juergen Habermas and Charles Taylor—do think of the task of philosophy in this way. But even Habermas and Taylor, who take Hegel seriously, and who find Dewey and Hook more plausible than do most analytic philosophers, share with the latter a suspicion that pragmatism goes too far in the direction of historicism, subjectivism, and relativism. Furthermore, in countries such as Germany and Italy, where philosophy did not go "analytic," pragmatism still looks a bit naive, a bit scientistic and reductionist.

Admirers of Dewey and Hook, however, feel that Taylor and Habermas are still reluctant to make what Hook, in the opening paragraph of this book, calls "the final break with the ancient and medieval outlook on the world." That break

---

3. Dewey, *Reconstruction in Philosophy,* vol. 12 of *The Middle Works of John Dewey,* p. 94.

is made, Hook thought, only when we stop trying either to reduce specifically human abilities and achievements to something lower or to explain these abilities and achievements by reference to something higher. To attempt the former is to remain in the grip of the Greek distinction between appearance and reality by insisting that the simpler and smaller (atoms, sub-atomic particles, neural processes) are somehow "realer" than the larger and more complex (moral decisions, works of art, political arrangements). To attempt the latter is to remain in the grip of the Greek and medieval idea that human beings can save themselves from despair only by envisaging a realm beyond time and chance—a realm of universal truth, absolute values, unconditional necessities.

Breaking with these older distinctions and ideas means taking Darwin seriously: refusing to attribute any ability to human beings that cannot be understood naturalistically as a product of evolution. But it also means avoiding reductionism—avoiding the idea that biology can somehow overrule culture. For Hook and Dewey, cultural evolution is biological evolution continued by other means. The enormous differences between past and present human communities illustrate the extraordinary flexibility of our species. This flexibility makes it pointless to argue that "human nature" dooms some proposed social experiment. There is nothing that biology, or any other natural science, or (for that matter) philosophy can tell us about ourselves that should make us hesitate to try such experiments.

Dewey's experimentalism is not scientistic. On the contrary, it treats the natural sciences as exemplary in their procedures, but as no more or less "in touch with reality" than politics or poetry.[4] The charge of being out of touch with reality is not one that a pragmatist can make, for that charge suggests that some aspect of human life could, per impossibile, be shielded from continual causal interaction with the environment. So a pragmatist will not criticize an opponent's position by saying that it is "merely subjective" but rather by saying that it is insufficiently useful, inappropriate to our present needs. The pragmatists' touchstone is never the intrinsic nature of reality, but always our current historical situation. So Dewey's or Hook's most fundamental criticism of Habermas's universalism and of Taylor's notion of "hypergoods" (human goods that are not historical products, not just for a time and a place) would not be that these notions are "unscientific" or "metaphysical" but rather that they do no useful work— that they distract us from the concrete social tasks at hand.

When we turn from changes in philosophical fashions to changes on the American political scene, two loom largest. The first is that the American left is no longer split, as it was in 1939, between the Communists and the social democrats. There are no Communists anymore. This is not just because Gorbachev dismantled Stalin's empire, but because the whole idea of state ownership of the means of production has been discredited, even in the eyes of those who think that market economies eventually produce unjust inequalities and think the welfare state a necessary remedy for such injustice.

As is evident in chapter 8 of this book ("The Good Society") Dewey and Hook were anti-Communist social democrats.

---

4. Here I am adopting an interpretation of Dewey that would be contested by other commentators. I argue the issue in exchanges with James Gouinlock, Thelma Lavine, and others in Herman Saatkamp, ed., *Rorty and the Pragmatists* (1995).

They split their time between fighting the Stalinists (who, in the late thirties, had corrupted large sectors of American intellectual and cultural life) and fighting anti-New Deal conservatives (who believed that the state must not be permitted to meddle with the market or to conduct "rash social experiments"). Both loathed the Communists' willingness to use "antifascism" as an excuse for turning a blind eye toward the crimes of the blood-soaked tyrant who then ruled Soviet Russia. Although both men distrusted FDR because he seemed to them not to go far enough, not to be sufficiently radical and experimental, they had no doubt that the alliance between the labor unions and the Democratic Party had helped to turn the country in the right direction.

The second big change in the American political scene is the emergence, among the intellectuals, of doubts about whether that *was* the right direction. In 1939, the intellectuals were, almost unanimously, on the left. In 1995 there is a significant, influential body of intellectuals who agree with the Republicans that "liberal" is a dirty word. These people idolize the market, urge the repeal of the welfare state, and are silent about the situation of the poor. Were they living today, I suspect that Dewey and Hook would split their time between making fun of the few remaining neo-Marxist radicals who still assume that nothing can really change until capitalism is overthrown, and excoriating the so-called "neoconservatives." These radicals, however, are a very minor concern, at least when compared with the clear and present dangers presented by the American Communist Party in 1939. So the vast bulk of both men's energies might have gone into reminding their fellow citizens of how bad things were in America before the Progressive Movement and the New Deal—before the beginnings of what we are now being asked to anathematize as "big government."

Hook and Dewey would have viewed the intellectuals who are urging us to take the United States back to where it was in 1900 with the same contempt with which they viewed the apologists for Stalin. Both men were intensely patriotic Americans—caught up in the romance of the American democratic experiment, intensely aware of themselves as the heirs of Jefferson and Emerson, Lincoln and Whitman, Eugene Debs and Jane Addams. Today's "neo-conservatives" would seem to them to be betraying everything that once made America an example to the world.

Pragmatism, considered as a set of philosophical doctrines about truth, knowledge, and value, is neutral between democratic and antidemocratic politics: no inferential links run from these doctrines to a concern with human suffering, or to a hope for greater social and political tolerance. But inference is one thing and motivation another. Dewey would never have bothered to formulate his philosophical doctrines had he not thought that their effect might be to break the grip of older ways of thinking upon his fellow citizens and to encourage them to undertake ever more radical social experiments. Hook would not have called Dewey "The Philosopher of American Democracy" (the title of the last chapter of this book, an allusion to Dewey's use of that phrase to describe Emerson) had he not been convinced that Dewey's pragmatism could be used as a tool to expand human freedom.

The affinity between pragmatism and political liberalism can be seen most clearly, perhaps, in the insistence, by those who now use "liberal" as a term of scorn, that we need to "return to traditional values" and that we need "moral absolutes." Dewey and Hook would have treated this as Aesopian language, as a disingenuous way of saying: don't think about how to diminish unnecessary human suffering, don't worry about how to change things so as to make people happier and freer, don't try to experiment. They would have seen the rhetoric of "traditional values" as a disguise for selfish unconcern.

It may be that Dewey and Hook witnessed, as Alan Ryan suggests in the title of his recent book, "the high tide of American liberalism." But if this is so, then America has lost its soul. Dewey and Hook were important philosophers, but their greatest importance was as exemplary Americans: Americans who, in the final words of this book, "still had hope for what America may yet be."

RICHARD RORTY
University of Virginia

JOHN DEWEY
An Intellectual Portrait

Chapter

I

THE MAN

THE philosophy of John Dewey represents a distinctive contribution to the thought of the modern age. He has carried to completion a movement of ideas which marks the final break with the ancient and medieval outlook upon the world. In his doctrines the experimental temper comes to self-consciousness. A new way of life is proposed to realize the ideal promise of our vast material culture. Organized intelligence is to take the place of myth and dogma in improving the common lot and enriching individual experience.

The consequences of every great advance in our knowledge of man and nature during the last few centuries are fused together in Dewey's comprehensive theory of experience. His leading conceptions are derived from the findings of modern biology, psychology, physics, and the historical sciences; his central faith is in the method of scientific inquiry by which these findings have been won. He has shown with patient detail that intelligence is at home in the natural world and not a mysterious intruder bringing its own standards from a realm beyond the skies. He has accepted the implications of a thoroughgoing naturalism for philosophy. By developing a theory of value based upon the responsibility of intelligence for the consequences of human choice, he has carried naturalism into the sacred precincts of morals. By applying the conclusions of a scientific analysis of morals, he has challenged the dominant social philosophies of our times.

John Dewey is America's philosopher not merely in virtue of his origins but in the fresh perspectives of his thought, and in his emphasis upon freedom, directed action, and scientific control. His writings have brought to reflective expression some of the most distinctive idioms of American faith and practice—its democratic traditions, its concern with methods and consequences, its sense of possibilities that are still open to courageous and disciplined intelligence.

In America's intellectual coming of age, no person has played a more important role than John Dewey. There is hardly a phase of American thought to which he has not made some contribution, hardly an aspect of American life which he has left uninterpreted. His influence has extended to the schools, the courts, the laboratories, the labor movement, and the politics of the nation. Despite their technical form all of Dewey's insights can be checked by the homely experience of the ordinary person whenever he is trying to find something out—provided only that he shows a dogged persistence in observing what he is doing and why.

Our concern in this study is primarily with John Dewey's ideas. Many are sure to ask, however: what manner of man is John Dewey, who at eighty is still so active and alive, in whom the wisdom of the sage combines so happily with a quiet zest and youthfulness of spirit? What were the environmental conditions under which his thought took shape? The curiosity is natural even if there be some dispute as to its philosophical relevance. A brief sketch of his background and the outstanding characteristics of both his personality and career may throw some light on his influence as well as the influences to which he has been subjected.

It is not merely symbolic that John Dewey was born in Vermont, developed his philosophy in Michigan, Minnesota, and Chicago, and brought his thought to a rounded completion in New York, the cultural metropolis of America. All early experience leaves its mark upon us, particularly in what we aspire to as well as in what we seek to escape from; but its heaviest deposit remains in our attitudes, in our immediate, even if unconscious, responses to typical situations and people. If John Dewey's early life and schooling in Vermont has a significant bearing upon his later intellectual development, it is not to be found in the character of the Vermont soil or climate, or the farming chores he performed to work his way through college. Much more pervasive in its influence was the character of the social life of the northern New England community in which John Dewey was reared. It was a community in which no great disparities in wealth or standards of living were to be found, and in which a man was judged, as the saying went, not by what he had but by what he did. The things a man did he did always a little differently from the way his neighbors did them. The differences were rarely so great that they imperiled the homogeneity of the culture. Nor were they such that they could not be controlled by the spontaneous pressure of a public opinion that protected the community from eccentricities without destroying them.

The Vermont and the New England of Dewey's boyhood and youth are gone. But he still carries with him the traces of its social environment, not as memories but as habits, deep preferences, and an ingrained democratic bias. They show themselves in his simplicity of manner, his basic courtesy, freedom from every variety of snobbism, and matter-of-course respect for the rights of everyone in America as a human being and a citizen. During the days when the Hoovers and Mellons were riding high, and making invidious distinctions between types of Americans, and appealing to the American way of life as a bulwark against social change, he remarked, "Where I was raised the Hoovers and the Mellons would have had a hard time passing for Americans."

Dewey's Americanism has never been nationalistic, like that of professional patriots, nor apologetic like that of our literary expatriates. Respectful of the cultures of other lands and peoples, he has a natural piety for the traditions in which he himself was cradled, even when he has reinterpreted them to meet the pressure of new needs and problems. After his educational mission to Japan at the end of the World War, his quiet refusal to accept the Order of the Rising Sun, the highest honor the Japanese government could bestow on a foreigner, was motivated by the feeling that to be a citizen of a democratic community was a sufficient political distinction for Americans.

The influence of the West—both the prairie land as well as the Windy City—was more momentous on Dewey's development. Here we do not have to guess, for we have it from Dewey himself that it was in this environment that he experienced the most urgent challenge, resulting in marked changes of thought. The community which he had left was a settled one in which traditions of use and wont, limited by the pattern of a comparatively simple economy, set the type of problems which men were called upon to face. But in Michigan and Minnesota sixty years ago, the soil had but newly been conquered for extensive cultivation. The great industrial boom was still a decade or more away. Social customs had not yet had time to cake into the familiar Eastern molds. The region was both an endpoint of the road from New England and a gateway to frontiers further north, west, and south. And this in more than a geographic sense. Problems were newer, more urgent. Changes and chances were greater; rewards for intelligent adaptation higher; the costs of ignorance and blundering more fateful. Here, practicality was not a matter of routine and thrift but of flexible action. Tomorrow took shape as a consequence of what was done or left undone today.

It was in this social environment that John Dewey abandoned all the old metaphysical lumber he had carried with him from the East and roughhewed the beams of a new philosophy. Nowhere was living so undeniably problematic. Nowhere did thinking and informed action make such an observable difference in their impact upon problems. The past was something to use here and now rather than a tradition to enjoy; the future something to create; the present a challenge to creation and construction. From the standpoint of the Midwest during the years of John Dewey's early maturity, it was easier to see that all experience was a succession of problems, that all faiths, philosophies, dogmas, had their origins in problems, and could be evaluated as

relevant or irrelevant, valid or invalid, only when their
problematic contexts had been uncovered.

At the University of Chicago, John Dewey developed
his new philosophy. Its vocabulary was so technical
that only a few of his fellow philosophers grasped its
revolutionary implications in their bearings on the traditional intellectual habits fostered by diverse philosophical schools. But among them was William James,
whose *Principles of Psychology* had been one of the
turning points in Dewey's philosophical development,
and who now welcomed Dewey as a peer. During his
stay at Chicago, Dewey carried his philosophy one step
further. It was a step destined to transform the whole
of American education. If knowledge involves doing,
then genuine learning can only be achieved by doing.
And if education be regarded as a process in which, by
controlled doing or experiment, certain attitudes, ideals,
and values are established as critical guides to action,
then it is possible to show that the basic problems of
both education and philosophy are the same. Paradoxical as it may sound, the esoteric doctrines which
Dewey discussed with his advanced postgraduate students were relevant to the larger problems which
emerged from the scientifically controlled practices he
introduced in the Laboratory School for children.

When he came to New York, John Dewey was already
a national figure. He found himself in a city which,
then as now, was the first center to feel the pull of
major social trends in the United States as well as to
register the winds of doctrine from all corners of the
world. From New York, he could see the ribbed structure of industry and finance extending itself over the
whole of America. Here was a vantage point from

which the increasingly important economic and political
problems could be studied in their concrete form. They
were problems that affected all other general problems
of American culture. They constituted a challenge to
his conception of philosophy and education which he
met in a way that no other American philosopher—
and for that matter, no other modern philosopher—has
done. Gradually, as the years went by, his influence
penetrated, directly through his students and their students, and indirectly through those who were reached
by his writings, to psychology, education, law, economics, sociology, politics, art, religion, and the philosophy of science. Even the professional philosophers
whose preoccupation with metaphysical and epistemological questions he had outflanked by demonstrating
that they could not be solved in their own terms, and
who had never failed both to honor and to disagree
with him, during the last twenty years have to a considerable extent reflected his influence. But Dewey has
always been ahead of his followers. In fact he has
been more interested in developing methods for the
co-operation of philosophers and scientists in the solution of problems than in enrolling followers or dis-
ciples. Since every man's philosophy, when he thinks
it through, is his own, Dewey expects that the philosophies of those who are in general agreement with him
will to an appreciable degree be different. At least in
emphasis; or in the form in which they tie the strands
of interest together. That is why so many who agree
with Dewey do not agree with each other.

At the close of the war, John Dewey became an international figure—the unofficial intellectual ambassa-
dor of the United States to the world. He was the

only living American philosopher and educator widely known outside of American borders. Wherever there were stirrings of new life and it was necessary to grapple with basic problems of education, requests were sent to him for counsel. Mexico, China, Japan, Russia, Turkey, South Africa were some of the countries which he visited on educational missions. It is interesting to observe that only to the extent that foreign nations were committed to the democratic way of life, could Dewey's educational theories be put into practice. The result is that only in the United States have they had institutional effect, and even here, not everywhere, nor in their full bearing.

Whether at home or abroad, John Dewey has remained the plain man from Vermont, the Midwestern democrat, and the subtle cosmopolitan with an enlightened world view.

Contemporary American culture has for so many years been under the influence of John Dewey that it is hard to realize that his philosophy has had a history. Not all of that history is relevant to his present philosophical position, nor all of the events which figure in the conventional chronicles of an educational career. But it is important to know that he developed out of a philosophical tradition which he helped to undermine, and to keep clearly in mind the phases of his early thought, if only to mark the distance he has come.

John Dewey was born in Burlington, Vermont, October 20, 1859, the year in which Darwin's *Origin of Species* was published. He dates his philosophic interest from the reading and study of Huxley's *Physiology*.

It was from this study that he derived a sense of the
interdependence and interrelated unity of things which
later on was to make the central features of Hegel's
thought appear so plausible to him.

During Dewey's student days, philosophy proper in
the United States was largely concerned with religious
and theological questions. This was less so at the
University of Vermont than elsewhere. But whatever
philosophy distinguished itself from religion, was nonetheless ancillary to it. The dominant philosophical
tradition was a variety of Scotch realism or intuitionism. According to the teachings of this school, the
basic ethical and logical ideas upon which all conduct
and demonstration depend, reveal their meaning, once
grasped, all at once. They are immediately recognized
as true in virtue of certain intuitive perceptions that
are natural to man; natural, in the sense that they are
original, not the result of education, history, custom, or
even reflection. These ultimate intuitions were thought
capable of yielding indisputable truths about existence,
such as, that an external world endures independently
of perception, that the self, as distinct from the organic body, was a real entity, that the relation of
causality was one of necessity, that God exists. In
short all the fundamental beliefs that appeared necessary for social and moral stability were declared to be
true in virtue of the immediate compulsion with which
they asserted themselves in our deeper intuition. In
this way they were safeguarded from skepticism, doubt,
and challenge.

As a young man Dewey did not go through the emotional crisis, provoked by the conflict of scientific truth
and revealed dogma, which was so typical of his gen-

eration. The religious atmosphere in which he grew
up both at home and in the community was liberal.
And there was a characteristic economy about Scotch
realism which prevented it from extending its intuitions
to the details of biblical history. Intellectual adjustments could therefore be made to the findings of science that were impossible to fundamentalism. The practical inadequacy of conventional creeds and rituals in
relation to his own personal experience, and to the
needs of others who had suffered some poignant tragedy, led Dewey to abandon institutional religion.

Interest in philosophy sixty years ago seemed to
point to a ministerial career, but Dewey was never
tempted by such a prospect. Upon graduation from
the University of Vermont, he taught high school for
two years in Oil City, Pennsylvania, during which time
he continued his philosophical reading. This was followed by a year's rural teaching in Charlotte, Vermont.
In the fall of 1882 he went to Johns Hopkins University to do graduate work. His resolution to devote
himself to philosophy was strengthened by the encouragement he received from William T. Harris, editor of
The Journal of Speculative Philosophy, America's first
major philosophical periodical. Harris had already
published several articles by Dewey which indicated impressive technical skill on the part of a young man of
twenty-two. At Johns Hopkins, Dewey listened to
Charles Peirce but did not come under his direct influence. Years later, after he had developed his own
distinctive ideas, Dewey was to return to the writings
of Peirce to find independent support for his philosophy of experimentalism. Dewey's own memories of
Peirce at Johns Hopkins center around some seminar

criticisms of atomic theories of consciousness. In them Peirce seemed to be suggesting a conception of the life of the mind as a series of flights and perches in the stream of consciousness, so brilliantly developed by James in his *Principles of Psychology*. Dewey completed his work for the doctorate with a dissertation on the *Psychology of Kant*.

During the next ten years, under the influence of George Sylvester Morris and the writings of the neo-Hegelian British school, especially those of T. H. Green, John Dewey made an intensive study of the works of Hegel. By making his own Hegel's insight that knowledge is never immediate or self-certifying, that every judgment has a ground, and that its truth or falsity depends upon something other than its own occurrence, Dewey liberated himself from the last vestiges of intuitionism. He never became an orthodox Hegelian, but his acquaintance with Hegel, as he himself states, left a permanent deposit on his thought, which will be apparent in subsequent chapters. The immediate appeal of Hegel to Dewey lay in Hegel's opposition to dualisms of all sorts, in his historical approach to all cultural life, his mastery of concrete material, and his extraordinarily acute perception of the continuities between matter and life, life and mind, mind and society. Dewey valued Hegel's method not for its arid pseudo deductions of one idea from another, nor as a substitute for scientific analysis, but as an approach which put one on guard against introducing into the thick stream of experience facile disjunctions, hard and fast alternatives, sharp separations. Some of these separations were a part of Dewey's New England heritage, which emphasized the division of the self from the world, of soul from body, of nature from God. Even in liberal evangelism these oppositions persisted. All schemes of redemption and salvation were ways of overcoming the separation between the natural —the imperfect and evil, and the supernatural—the perfect and good.

The "inward laceration" which Dewey testifies to feeling as a consequence of this dualism was eased and lifted by a philosophy which taught that the world was just as necessary to God as God to the world, matter to form as form to matter, the body to the spirit as spirit to body. What seemed from a theological perspective to be a natural evil—the life of impulse, passion, and action—appeared now to be a natural condition for the achievement of good. The function of discipline in any area of experience was not merely to curb but to liberate power for significant purposes. Every belief became subject to test; but there was no standard of testing so high, no intuition so deep, that it was not itself subject to further test in subsequent experience. Even after Dewey abandoned Hegelian idealism and its artificial schematisms, he honored Hegel's insight into the processes of change out of which the relative and shifting concretions of things emerge that provide the context of all discourse and action. He naturalized Hegel's historical approach by a biological theory of mind and an institutional analysis of social behavior.

Dewey's drift from Hegelianism was gradual. His experiences at Michigan and Minnesota had led him to see that reason, which Hegel had asserted to be an intrinisic feature of existence, was something to be achieved in action, not something which was presup-

posed by action. Where reason makes a difference, it
is as intelligence, not as embodied structure, and not
as a metaphysical trait which all things possess over
and above their physical, biological, and social qualities. For Hegel, the world, properly understood, was
already ideal, so that there was no rational way of
choosing between different ideals in any concrete situation. The better ideal in this view was not one which
proved itself in the light of foreseen consequences but
one which established itself by power of sheer survival.

Such a conception of reason and the ideal could not
long withstand challenge in a world which people strove
to make more reasonable and to render more ideal. By
the time Dewey was called to the University of Chicago
in 1894, he had come to question the relevance of any
metaphysical view of the nature of reason and ideals to
specific problems, difficulties, and predicaments. For
the latter demanded applied intelligence, tools, techniques, a knowledge acquired piecemeal by methods
which were self-corrective precisely because they made
no presumptuous claims to absoluteness or finality.

As director of the Experimental School of Chicago,
Dewey was able by a kind of laboratory practice to test
his ideas of the nature of intelligence, its role in human
behavior, and the differential effects on human growth
its presence or absence involves.

The Dewey Laboratory School was the most important experimental venture in the whole history of
American education. It has a story of its own which
has been ably told by Mayhew and Edwards in their
book on *The Dewey School*. Long before "progressive
education" became a movement or even an identifying
phrase, its basic principles were experimentally devel-

oped in a short period of seven years by people whose
original concern had been the education of their own
children, but, on scientific as well as social grounds, soon
became interested in the education of every child. An
imposing galaxy of scientists and philosophers from
the University of Chicago co-operated in elaborating
the curriculum, adapting it to various age levels, and
also in teaching. Among them were the geologist,
Chamberlin, originator of the planetesimal hypothesis
of the earth's origin; Michelson, the physicist; Coulter,
in botany; Whitman, in zoology; Jacques Loeb, in
physiology; A. Smith, in chemistry; W. I. Thomas, in
sociology; and G. H. Mead, J. H. Tufts, and J. R.
Angell, in philosophy.

The problems of education for Dewey were an opportunity to develop and test ideas which in the first instance were not technically educational at all. From
this time on, however, he sought to link his philosophical activity more directly with concrete subject matters. More and more, the central tasks of philosophy
for Dewey were questions of meaning, method, and inquiry in relation to specific problems of the arts and
sciences. Soon he came to regard the form in which
the traditional problems of metaphysics were expressed
as largely the result of misinterpretations of the nature of inquiry. His lifework now consisted in ex-
ploring the possibility that the rationale of scientific
inquiry, whose results in some fields had already transformed the face of the globe, could be employed in the
solution of all problems of human experience.

This point of view naturally involved a break with
traditional and current conceptions of philosophy, although not with all the traditional and current prac-

tices of philosophy. This will be made manifest in Dewey's conception of philosophy.

It is difficult to speak of the personal qualities of John Dewey without lapsing into the language of eulogy. Eulogy is not always an aid to clarity; nor does John Dewey need it. The objective record of this life and thought is sufficient to give an adequate impression of the character of his personality. Few philosophers have said so little of themselves. His writings contain hardly any hints that are autobiographical. The depth and richness of his personal experience may be inferred from his sensitive analysis of psychological processes wherever these are relevant to his main theme. But his gaze and interest seem always directed outward to common problems, public situations, and the larger frames of reference which unite multitudes in social traditions, social concerns, and predicaments. If William James may be called the philosopher of the underdog, John Dewey is surely the philosopher of the plain man—of the millions who are neither on top nor on bottom, for whom life is not a prolonged holiday or a romantic protest but a succession of problems, at work, at war, or at home. Concerned, to be sure with individuals, his interest is not in the special case, whether labeled errant genius, or problem child, or *the* individual, but with conditions and problems that affect multitudes of individuals. For him every individual is a special case.

Everyone acquainted with John Dewey knows that he is the least awesome person in the world. He would never be picked out in a crowd either for quality of

voice, gait, or bearing. There is an air of restful and
mild-mannered sensitiveness about him which has led
someone guessing his identity to say that he looked like
a cross between a philosophical anarchist and Robert
Louis Stevenson. In his relationship with people he is
unassuming, sometimes almost to the point of efface-
ment. His simplicity, directness, and complete lack of
self-consciousness puts even the shyest person at his
ease, and yet leads him to do more things and to do
them better than he ordinarily would. His intellectual
humility is so profound that it might seem to be a pose
affected by a great man were it not so obviously sincere. Whether it is a farmer or teacher, storekeeper
or factory worker, public official or student, he exchanges ideas with them as if he were the learner, or
both were learners in a common enterprise. Wherever
John Dewey and someone else are present, there we
have an intellectual community. He has a sense for
what is authentic and original in every person's experience and a way of inducing the self-confidence
which is a pre-requisite for its adequate telling.

Deeply appreciating books and the book-learned, he
treasures most the reflective articulation of those who
have grappled with problems first hand. The ideas of
a roving typesetter, a farm hand in Minnesota, a re-
tired schoolteacher in Mississippi, a refugee from
European terror, receive the same sympathetic attention as the technical writings of a colleague. Sometimes more. Praise embarrasses him, but he suffers
contradiction and qualification easily. He has never
been impressed by a title or degree; and, as certain
foreign governments have learned, honors and junket
tours will never persuade him to deviate a hairbreadth

from what he considers his intellectual and moral responsibility in the face of available evidence.

To three generations of students—even to his critics—John Dewey's encouragements have always been generous; sometimes too much so. But there is a great teacher's wisdom in it. Criticism, he believes, should not wither the sources of creative insight. Before men can produce significant things, they must first produce. Achievements and discoveries are processes of growth, rarely do they spring into existence as flawless creations. A deep insight may sometimes be defended by wrong reasons. In such cases, it is at least as important to hold on to and develop the insight as to discard the reasons. John Dewey has the rare gift, without the slightest trace of condescension, of making men believe in themselves, of giving them confidence in the adventure of ideas, therewith strengthening their desire to learn and reflect in order to act intelligently.

Despite his gentleness there is a deep vein of Vermont marble in his character. None have been so shocked as those who have mistaken this gentleness for softness. In controversy he does not give ground easily and hesitates not at all in getting rough with opponents whose good faith he has reason to challenge whether they are ambassadors or newspaper columnists. Once aroused, he holds on tenaciously until things come to a decision. There is an intellectual toughness about him and an emotional ease under attack which indicate complete inner self-confidence.

One of the most impressive traits of John Dewey is his intellectual and physical vigor. The quality of his

thought seems to improve with age. Even his critics
grant that his most recent books have constituted his
weightiest and most systematic statement of the philosophy of experimentalism. An active curiosity and
willingness to learn lead him to test his formulations by
continuous application to new material. The pat
phrase, the polished line, the stereotypes of a fixed
system he leaves to others. At seventy he wrote that
his philosophy "was still too much in process of change
to lend itself to [definitive] record." At eighty, he is
at work on several new books, having published seven
and completely revised two others during the last decade. Every volume that has appeared represents the
result of various drafts. He can easily write a chapter
a day, ranging in length from five to seven thousand
words. And the next day discard it and begin all over
again. Some of his best analyses of specific problems
have never been published since he does not revise but
rewrites from scratch.

He is capable of a concentration so intense that only
a physical interruption of the most literal sort can dis-
turb him. His own explanation of his working habits
is that there was no other way of getting anything
done, while bringing up a large family on a modest in-
come, than by developing an insensitiveness to the noise
and distractions of a happy household. His physical
vitality is no less astonishing. He seems to rely more
on a tough New England constitution than on overcoat
or rubbers in the stormiest weather. When he is interested, he can sit through meetings and discussions from
morning to night without showing more fatigue than
men half of his age. His absent-mindedness, which is
usually the result of preoccupation with ideas, has

given rise to many amusing situations and tales. Sometimes negligent in small things, he never loses sight of
the main issues. His sense of humor is delightful, although a little unpredictable. A dry chuckle, a grin,
a twinkle that lights up the whole face are its premoni-
tory signs. His low and husky voice does not alter its
tone whatever the occasion. It has brought relief to
more than one insomniac among his students and bored
many who came not to hear a teacher but to enjoy a
showman. But after one had learned to listen, there
was sufficient recompense in the freshness of his thinking and the challenge of his leading ideas. "You could
actually *see* him think," Ernest Nagel has aptly said
in recalling his student days. And there is at least one
witness who can testify to the accuracy of the charming
picture that Irwin Edman paints in his *Philosopher's
Holiday* of John Dewey in the classroom.

Always carefully prepared before he came to class,
Dewey would seem to be making a fresh start when he
began to lecture. There was something unconsciously
optimistic about the literal way he took the ideals of
graduate instruction. For he would never spend time
in motivating interest or attention. Once, after spend-
ing three consecutive hours on the analysis of the
meaning of the word "this," he tentatively concluded
with the remark "I think this is a little clearer to me
now." He was a little perplexed at the amusement of
the class, most of whose members had never imagined
that there was anything problematic about "this" except why Dewey was discussing it.

The same scrupulous desire to do justice to all aspects of a question accounts for some of the qualities
of his style—that scapegoat of all impatient critics.

A kind of tradition has grown up about the difficulties of his style; and it is undeniable that his most original writing is the hardest to read. Yet there are many passages in Dewey that are comparable to the best philosophical prose in the language. Where he is restating a position already won, Dewey's style has a grace and flexible vigor that carry easily a rich freightage of ideas. One need mention only *Human Nature and Conduct, Reconstruction in Philosophy,* and impressive portions of *Experience and Nature* and *Art as Experience.* It is when he is grappling with a problem and working his way toward a solution that his writing becomes involved and overqualified. In part this is due to a desire to meet objections in advance; in part, to an attempt to escape the treachery of words that carry over connotations derived from other contexts. Until the analysis is complete, one does not see where Dewey is coming out. When a conclusion has been reached, it is sometimes so breathtaking that it is necessary to retrace the steps in the argument to see how it was prepared for in the apparently innocent comments at the outset. The late Justice Oliver W. Holmes would remark about Dewey's *Experience and Nature* that in reading its every page he had the overwhelming conviction that he was reading a great book even though he could not always say why.

Even those who are not acquainted with his writings know by the contexts in which his name appears in public print that wherever there is a progressive cause to be defended, John Dewey is always in the front ranks. His progressivism is a philosophy not a sentiment. But it is rooted in a sentiment which burns fiercely against cruelty and injustice no matter under what banner they seek to hide. Whether it is a fish peddler who has been arrested on trumped-up charges, a newspaper-stand owner whose franchise and living have been sacrificed by a bureaucratic error, a negro who faces a legal lynching, a labor organizer persecuted for legitimate activities, a teacher in jeopardy because of his heretical ideas, a Communist indicted for his opinions rather than for a specific crime, a victim of a poisonous slander campaign organized by the Communist Party and its dupes, a refugee marked for assassination by the GPU or Gestapo—John Dewey has always given freely of his time, his sympathies, and his effort. He has been attacked as Public Enemy No. 1 by every pressure group which has something to conceal, by every organization which seeks to deprive others of the privileges it demands for itself. For him no case is ever closed if a human being has unjustly suffered. He is surprised at others' surprise that he should give so much of himself to remedying evils in which he is not personally involved, and to fighting for the right of a hearing for causes in which he has no belief. These are to him the elementary obligations of every democrat whose faith rests not on consoling lies but on all the relevant and available truth. He undertakes these activities because he lives as he thinks.

He was a pioneer in organizing teachers in behalf of better living conditions, better schools, and better teaching. He was an important figure in the Teachers Union in New York until it fell under political control. Whereupon, together with the original founders of the Union, he organized the Teachers Guild. In one capacity or another he has been associated with every movement to organize a Farmer-Labor Party during the last generation. Together with S. O. Levinson, he led the American movement for the Plan to Outlaw War. After 1929, the League of Independent Political Action and the People's Lobby, of which he was chairman, helped to arouse the nation to a sense of its responsibility in relation to the problem of relief and unemployment, regarded at that time as the appropriate objects of private philanthropy.

The struggle for civil liberties is accepted by Dewey as a matter of course in a world in which democracy must be made safe *here* and *now* as the condition precedent of extending it elsewhere. In this struggle he has never grown tired, has never retreated, has never yielded to moods of helplessness before the victory of brute power. He helped organize the American Civil Liberties Union as well as the American Association of University Professors and is a member of defense and educational organizations too numerous to list here.

Of all the defense causes in which John Dewey has been interested, two made the greatest impression upon him. The first was the Sacco-Vanzetti case. He was convinced of the innocence of these humble men; he was also convinced that the authorities would never dare, in the face of the evidence, to let them die. During their last days, he himself was overwhelmed by a personal family tragedy which prevented him from joining those who picketed the death house in which they lay. The news of their death came as a great shock. He never again placed faith in the willingness of those who were in high place to reverse themselves when they were in error. His devastating analysis of the report of the Lowell Commission, behind which Governor Fuller hid, is a classic illustration of logic in action.

The second cause was the case of Leon Trotsky. No more than in the case of Sacco-Vanzetti, did Dewey share Trotsky's political views. But he noticed that many self-avowed "liberals" remained silent when Trotsky was deprived of his right to political asylum, even when his very life was jeopardized, although they vociferously protested against the slightest discriminatory measures against adherents of Stalin anywhere. What was worse, they refused to examine the evidence which Leon Trotsky presented to substantiate his claim that he was the victim of the most monstrous frame-up in history. When a committee of American scholars, educators, and labor leaders was organized to defend Trotsky's right of asylum, and to investigate the truth of the charges made against him, it became the object of a systematic campaign of defamation. It was at this point that Dewey began to take a very serious interest in the entire proceedings.

He headed a Commission of Inquiry into the Moscow Trials and after almost two years of close study and investigation of the evidence, helped write the findings which completely exonerated Trotsky and his son from the charges made against them. More than ever, now, was he opposed to the theoretical presuppositions of Leninism, Trotskyism, and Stalinism. But he had kept faith with his own ideals—with the best American ideals—of freedom of inquiry and justice, even to those with whom we disagree.

It is difficult to evaluate the extent of John Dewey's intellectual influence on American life in quantitative terms. Many of his ideas have become so much a part

of the cultural climate of our time that those who hold
them are not always aware of their source. The daring
vision of yesterday is the commonplace of today, and
normally we should expect the younger generation to
read Dewey with the feeling that they "knew it all the
time." The amazing thing, however, is that Dewey has
made a greater impression upon the younger men of
each decade since the turn of the century than he has
upon his own strict contemporaries. One of the reasons
for this is the suggestiveness of his writings. Few things
are worked out with detailed finish or with the finality
and elegance of a mathematical demonstration.   But in
recompense a host of suggestions flock to the mind of
the reader from the pages of his books. Another reason
for his appeal is that he seems to have anticipated, and
in some measure to have been directly responsible for,
several latter-day tendencies in the philosophy of science, including the social sciences. Even more significant is the fact that his emphasis upon intelligent
action has made him the natural ally of all enemies of
obscurantism in its perpetual wars against enlightenment. It is safe to predict that with the resurgence of
fanaticisms and political absolutisms, Dewey's ideas
will still have an arresting quality of challenge for a
long time to come.

John Dewey has always denied that his philosophy
constituted a system. He has poked good-natured fun at
the German professor who strung a series of polysyl-
labic isms together to describe the pragmatic movement
in philosophy. And if by system is meant starting with a few axiomatic ideas and logically deducing
a set of doctrines for all fields of experience, and then
imposing these doctrines upon the ready-made materials

supplied by other investigators, Dewey's philosophy, of course, is not a system.

A philosophy, however, may have a systematic quality without being a system in the above sense. That is to say, as it explores different fields, the central insights, methods, and conclusions of one field may hang together with those of other fields in such a way that they mutually provide some supporting force and evidence in relation to each other. For example, a preconceived theory of mind which deduces what thought must be in different fields independently of the procedures by which we empirically establish the presence of thinking in those fields, can be called a system of mind. An empirical investigation of mind in a particular field which leads to conclusions that reappear when fresh investigations of other fields are conducted gives us a systematic theory of mind. It is in this last sense that I believe Dewey's philosophy is systematic. The subsequent chapters are offered by way of partial evidence. The scope of Dewey's intellectual interests is so comprehensive that insofar as his philosophy is systematic it expresses a philosophy of life. In this respect, and in this respect alone, although it is not philosophy in the grand manner, it is still philosophy in the grand tradition.

Chapter

II

PHILOSOPHY AND CULTURE

IN no other field of human thought has the claim to
the possession of absolute truth been made so often
as in philosophy—a fact to which its history from
Plato to Aquinas, from Descartes to Husserl bears eloquent witness. Yet in no field has there been so little
agreement as to what these truths are.

Even religion shows a larger measure of common
belief and fewer basic divisions than does philosophy.
For philosophic disagreement extends not only to specific conclusions and the methods of attaining them but
to what constitutes the very subject matter of philosophy itself. This scandalous situation is not altogether
unique to philosophy, for a similar state of affairs is
observable among some of the social disciplines, particularly those that are undeveloped and unscientific.
But philosophers, even more so than social scientists,
have been given to settling questions about the nature
of their subject matter by ruling one another beyond
the pale with arbitrary definitions of what philosophy
is. Since these definitions reflect the particular kind of
philosophy to which the philosopher is already committed, little progress has been made. Considerable
skepticism has thereby been evoked among intelligent
laymen of the whole philosophic enterprise. The dis-
parity between promise and performance has been so
glaring that philosophy seems to be but a name for

the elaboration of personal prejudices masquerading as impersonal axioms.

John Dewey has sought to avoid this fruitless clash of definitions by first asking in humble, empirical fashion: What, as a matter of historical fact, has philosophy been? What does an analysis of philosophy as intellectual behavior show? On the basis of an inquiry into what philosophers in their writings have actually done, of the generating problems around which they have organized their doctrines, and of the subsequent career of those doctrines, Dewey makes a *proposal* to those who distinguish themselves as philosophers to conceive of philosophy in a certain way. He believes that this proposal, if acted upon, is more likely to lead to fruitful results than any other.

There is nothing circular in this approach. One does not have to accept Dewey's proposal at the outset to follow his historical inquiry, although the outcome of that inquiry will have a bearing upon the reasonableness of the proposal. For, despite the fact that there is no agreement on definitions of philosophy, there is virtual unanimity as to what writings of the past are philosophical, and consequently what thinkers are philosophers.

What does investigation of the history of philosophy show? According to Dewey, philosophies have primarily been concerned with the defense or criticism of certain ways of life, belief, and action in the culture of which they are a part. No matter what one thinks philosophy *should* be, most systems of philosophy, especially those that have been accepted as official or proscribed as heretical, have in fact been phases of patterns of cultural behavior, bearing on their face the characteristics

of the age in which they were conceived. Philosophies
have articulated with greater nicety and insight the
beliefs, interests, and modes of feeling of different
groups struggling for mastery over nature and each
other. Where a philosophy has cosmic sweep and
makes claims to universality, it can easily be shown that
its attempt to render all of existence significant is undertaken from the local and temporal perspective of
some selected feature of the life of its own times.

The individual philosopher is not always aware of
this; but the uses to which his philosophy is put, the
character of the groups which range themselves around
it in advocacy or opposition, its influence on education
in schools and without, indicate that, whatever else
philosophies may be, they are rationalizations (in both
senses of the term) or criticisms of what people believe, hope, or do. They therefore have a bearing upon
conduct, and a practical influence on affairs, even when
they boast of their impracticality.

The relationships between the history of philosophy
and the problems of cultural change and conflict, although intimate, do not lie open to every eye. They
are obscured by the fact that most philosophers begin
their studies out of the books of other philosophers,
speak a technical language specially created to deal
with what are called philosophical problems *per se,*
and tend to translate and reinterpret problems of contemporary culture into terms and categories devised
by their predecessors. There is also the fact that some
philosophers, although not the major ones, seem to be
completely oblivious to social issues of any kind, and
are occupied exclusively with questions of space, time
and eternity, matter and motion, substance and cause.

And even among the major philosophers, certain of their writings seem to have precious little to do with basic attitudes and beliefs.

Part of this seeming irrelevance is to be accounted for by the fact that some philosophers, like Descartes and Leibnitz, have been physicists and mathematicians, and others, like Locke and Kant, psychologists. Their contributions to the history of science can be easily differentiated from their contributions to the history of philosophy. But there still remains a huge bulk of doctrines that belong to no field of science and yet do not *obviously* fall within the scope of Dewey's hypothesis about the nature of past philosophy. It is in his analysis of precisely these apparently unrelated philosophical doctrines that Dewey has won the major evidence for his view. According to him, a closer examination of the cultural context of philosophical reflection reveals that problems of belief and value are to be found, with varying degrees of complexity, in every field of philosophy, no matter how far removed it seems to be at first blush from mundane affairs. For purposes of convenient exposition, we may distinguish these fields as the ethical, the logical and epistemological, and the metaphysical.

When men choose between alternatives of action, not blindly, but after reflection, they give reasons to themselves or others, for the choices made. If the choice is between modes of conduct in the sphere of personal or social morality, even ordinary usage distinguishes between knowledge and wisdom. Wisdom is the proper use of knowledge in human affairs. "The wise man" and "the philosopher" are expressions often employed interchangeably; and, etymologically, philosophy is the love

of wisdom. Yet, despite the fact that knowledge and
wisdom are distinguished from each other, they are related. One may know and not be wise but one cannot
be wise and ignorant. Whoever justifies one course of
conduct as wiser than another assumes that there are
grounds and reasons in knowledge for the choice. At
the very first level on which abstract philosophy emerges
from the impact of practical issues, it asks: What,
then, are the place and role of knowledge and reason
in the conduct of life? This question is inescapable as
soon as we seek to understand our choice, to defend our
method of reaching it, and to reassure ourselves or to
persuade others that we have chosen wisely.

To this extent almost every intelligent person on
some occasions is philosophical. The professional philosopher differs at this point from others only in the degree of his absorption in the general problem of the
definition of the good and its relation to reason and
knowledge. He differs from others in kind when he asks:
In virtue of what properties are knowledge and reason
able to perform their office of control and regulation
of choice? What does it mean to have knowledge? What
does it mean to be reasonable? Or, as Dewey puts it,
the second level of philosophical sophistication is the
one on which we ask: What are the constitution and
structure of knowledge and reason in virtue of which
they perform their assigned function? The answers
philosophers have made, we do not have to consider
here. Most of them assume that it is in virtue of some
superior quality, almost magical, that reason can order
life and introduce within it a coherent plan. But
Dewey's point is that the reference to the exigencies of
ordinary experience is still there, even if it is indirect.

And he is prepared to show that in any given cultural milieu, conflicting theories of the nature of knowledge and reason can be significantly correlated with conflicting series of grounds and reasons offered to justify different solutions of basic social and personal questions.

Knowledge is something that human beings are said to have; and reason is what they profess to follow. No matter what the qualities are by which we mark knowledge off from ignorance, and reason from impulse, it is possible to ask: What in the nature of things makes it possible to achieve wisdom, based as it is on knowledge and reason: what properties must the world antecedently possess in order to make one mode of thought or action "truer" or "better" than another? Such questions are raised by metaphysicians in many variant forms. The problem at the basis of all speculative metaphysics, says Dewey, is: "What is the constitution of nature, of the universe, which renders possible and guarantees the conception of knowledge and of good that are reached?" Here, too, the reference to problems of life and conduct is present, although more indirect; here, too, there is a high positive correlation between the type of metaphysical construction accepted as an answer to questions of the sort given above, and the character of the practical decisions adopted or approved in social and personal affairs.

For Dewey, the practical and intellectual motives which drive men to ask these metaphysical questions are intelligible; the questions as put and the answers as given are not. It *is* legitimate to ask: What is the history and nature of the world in which we must live out our lives? But this question is one that only science can answer. Science does not trade in certainties, nor does it derive trustworthy values from the structure of the physical world, not to speak of guaranteeing them. Traditional metaphysics has always been a violent and logically impossible attempt to impose some parochial scheme of values upon the cosmos in order to justify or undermine a set of existing social institutions by a pretended deduction from the nature of Reality. The very use of the term "Real" in the writings of all metaphysicians indicates that it is a value term. Since neither scientific method nor knowledge can absolutely vouchsafe the desired values and beliefs, metaphysics must claim to be a royal road to a higher kind of knowledge than empirical science can ever reach, and to be in the possession of insights and methods of superior validity.

It is not surprising, then, that the techniques and vocabulary which the philosopher brings to the discussion of all these problems, particularly those which Dewey calls epistemological and metaphysical, are highly specialized, and at first glance seem irrelevant to fundamental attitudes of personal and social life. Like all those who live by using words, philosophers have a technical pride and tradition. But once crack the shell of any metaphysical doctrine, what appears is not verifiable knowledge but a directing bias. The philosopher, according to Dewey's hypothesis, insofar as he is not discussing, unbeknown to himself, problems of psychology, physics, or biology, is always discussing the basic beliefs of his time or his own life, and trying to find grounds to justify them. These basic beliefs are *of* his time but not necessarily *about* them. They may be about the nature of good, evil, God, and salvation.

The history of philosophy is Dewey's evidence for this view. As he reads it, what gives meaning to the metaphysical and epistemological conflicts of Greek, medieval, and modern philosophy are conflicting evaluations of cultural change. The misty and vague abstractions of philosophic systems are remote only in form from the vivid and concrete problems of social experience. Why should the controversy over universals, over innate ideas, over the unity of the self, over free will, over the relative place of sensation and reason in knowledge, over the general will, the nature of law, determinism, and sovereignty, have stirred up not only the Schools but the Church, Court, State, and sometimes even the Market Place? The history of philosophy, as distinct from the history of science, is not a record of objectively verifiable reports about the nature of the world and man's place in it, but a record of judgments of interpretation and practical direction. The strife of systems appears as a manifestation of the strife of cultures, of the struggle of different groups within the same culture, and of visions born of personal differences within groups.

In the light of the foregoing, it should be clear what Dewey means when he claims that the pre-eminent subject matter of philosophy has been the relation between things and *values*. What things are and how they are organized in relation to each other is the generic subject matter of science. What *values* are, how they are derived and justified, and their place in organizing experience into a coherent pattern, is the generic concern of the philosopher. Directly or indirectly, every philosopher has projected or criticized a survey of the world from the standpoint of some value or interest.

It is this and only this aspect of his thought which gives the philosopher a distinctive and legitimate subject matter. Any other view makes of philosophy either a pretentious substitute for science, or a kind of dark, poetic venture, or a strictly formal analysis of language. The history of philosophy shows that at different times it has been all these and perhaps other things as well; but it also shows that its predominant theme—and one which has given it a continuity that no other conception of philosophy can account for—has been the relation between "the real" and "the ideal," between "what is" and "what ought to be," between "what exists" and "what should or should not exist."

Philosophers, of course, have not been the only ones to concern themselves with values. During the last fifty years sociologists and historians have undertaken scientific studies of the conditions under which certain values appear and disappear. What, then, is the difference between the philosopher and the social historian? According to Dewey, the difference is this: The historian or sociologist takes values as social facts on the same basis as other social facts, investigates their distribution and institutional expressions, establishes correlations between certain clusters of values and other social and nonsocial factors—all in the hope of finding a formula which will enable him to predict the type of values that will flourish in determinate societies and vice versa. The philosopher is interested in the evaluation of values, in an analysis of what passes for valuable in order to ascertain whether it is truly judged as valuable. Insofar as his evaluation is intelligent, he will take into account everything relevant that the historian or sociologist can tell him about the causes, contexts, and consequences of values; but he does not take these values as simply given but as controls of policy to be themselves controlled by subsequent analysis and action. The philosophic approach to values is not merely descriptive but normative. What human beings do when they deliberate on alternatives of personal conduct, the philosopher systematically does in relation to the major alternatives of social policy.

So far we have been presenting Dewey's conception of the role of philosophy in the history of thought. We now come to his proposal of the role philosophy should play in the world today. His proposal is that philosophers should do consciously what until now they have done in the main unconsciously and, therefore, badly. His program for philosophers is that they directly confront the major problems and beliefs of our society, make explicit our value assumptions, project alternatives of social choice, investigate methods of investigation, formulate a theory of inquiry that may aid in overcoming intellectual confusions, and furnish, if possible, intelligent grounds of action in meeting the times and its troubles. Wherever fundamental problems of evaluation are to be considered, there is the post for a philosopher, not because he has the answers but because he has a critical theory of what constitutes a possible answer and why. And since the problems of social evaluation are more fundamental than any others, in the sense that whatever attitude we take to them has the most pervasive influence on the attitudes taken elsewhere (a proposition which will later be proved), they constitute the pre-eminent posts of honor and battle for philosophers.

Such a proposal may seem on a first hearing to be

a call to philosophy to abandon its detachment, its universal scope, and its analytic rigor. This as we shall see is no more justified than the fear expressed by some philosophers that such a proposal is an invitation to philosophers to give up their vocation and devote themselves to glorified social work. To all who speak in this way, the rejoinder can properly be made that most of what has passed for philosophy until now and presumably represents an alternative conception of philosophy, has never shown critical detachment, has been universal in phrase but always partisan in interest and emphasis, and has been as loose in its methods of reasoning as it has been silly in its conclusions. Nor does this proposal invite philosophers to turn into evangelical social reformers or philanthropists but rather to acquire mastery over some specific subject matter in the social field and test by concrete investigation the values, beliefs, and methods on which policies in these fields rest.

Values and beliefs, it has been said, constitute the subject matter of philosophy; philosophical activity is the *criticism* of values and beliefs. It has also been said that the subject matter of philosophy, since it is supplied by the social life of man, can be investigated from the standpoint of the special sciences. What remains as distinctive of philosophy and as constituting its unique influence, for good or evil, on social affairs, is its *critical evaluation of values and beliefs*. This is an office and function to which no other discipline aspires.

But, it may be asked, in what way is the method of criticism distinctive or unique to philosophy? Are not all the arts and sciences critical? Have they not, already in use, methods of criticizing the work done in their respective fields? Must their practitioners wait on philosophy to be able to criticize theories, books, plays, pictures, and the actions of their fellow men? Certainly not. Dewey grants that discriminating judgment in any field is a form of criticism. But as a rule these criticisms are made on the basis of implicit assumptions, themselves accepted as valid without benefit of critical evaluation. Conduct is criticized from the standpoint of some law, custom, or religious code; a picture, by certain standards which are set by habit, authority, or fashion; a theory, in the light of a conventional schema of verification or of its coherence with other accepted theories. It is only when the method or standard of criticism on this first level is contrasted with other methods or standards, and the grounds for choosing between them made explicit and subjected, if there is need for it, to further evaluation, that criticism is philosophical. That is why Dewey sometimes defines philosophy as a criticism of methods of criticism.

How does such a method proceed? Primarily by the clarification of meanings—a process in which their contexts are laid bare, their operational correspondences established, their implications and consistencies explored, and their obscurities and ambiguities reduced. Many of the terms employed with a free and easy familiarity in discourse have a vague and rough meaning. This is particularly true of the terms that are called basic or fundamental in special fields of inquiry, and of almost all terms which express evaluations and appraisals. Whether we are interested in enjoying meanings or verifying them, clarification increases the scope of appreciation and the precision of understanding.

Clarification of meanings involves a critique of certain language habits which have burdened men in their attempt to solve problems, and resulted in pseudo problems in whose fruitless pursuit immense energies have been misdirected. For example, many philosophers who have admitted that there is no scientific warrant for separating mind from body often speak of mind as if it exercised an influence as a separate force upon behavior and wrestle with a problem their own linguistic habits have created. We know that all interactions into which a thing enters exhibit its nature but in our language *the* nature of a thing is often referred to as a substance in which qualities inhere and which presumably has a character in independence of its interactions, thus generating another set of insoluble problems. In all fields many people are unable to interpret the abstractions they use because they cannot indicate what controls in inquiry may be applied to them. The result of the use of unanalyzed and unanalyzable abstractions is that, despite heated controversies, issues that are fateful for the life of the community are rarely joined in a manner which permits of intelligent agreement or difference.

Philosophic criticism is not only a process of clarifying and discriminating meanings: it suggests and unifies meanings. In making us aware of what we intend or desire, it introduces some order into our basic choices and commitments, makes us review alternatives previously ignored or glossed over, multiplies the possibilities to be considered, and by a kind of anticipatory enactment of the future lessens regret and repentance. Although philosophy does not pretend to discover new truths about the nature of the world and man, it facilitates the quest for such discovery by both suggesting and refining new points of view. As Dewey conceives it, philosophical criticism does not clip the wings of vision but, by making it responsive to what may be achieved, lends it power.

Questions about trustworthy belief do not arise only in social inquiry, although they are conspicuously present there. They arise wherever evaluations are made. In every field of human knowledge there is a point where we find ourselves thrown back upon a belief in one method or assumption, rather than another, in behalf of which we cannot offer the same kind of evidence as we accept for the conclusions that have been reached by this method or assumption. For example, the principles which guide the processes of confirmation cannot themselves be confirmed by the same procedure. Why do we believe them? Why, indeed, do we put our faith in scientific methods of resolving problems rather than in nonempirical methods? Why do we operate with one form of implication rather than another? All of the fundamental assumptions of any science or logic are of the nature of decisions. But are these decisions merely prejudices, arbitrarily put on or off? Do we not, in the specific fields in which they are made, regard them as more trustworthy, as better than others? Do we not give some grounds for our choice? And if there is a choice, are we not engaged in evaluating between basic alternatives? The scientist may ignore such evaluations, but the philosopher cannot. Although the whole problem has never been adequately explored, it is at least an open question whether the grounds we offer for reasonable and trustworthy belief of "basic" assumptions in the field of science are not of the same generic character as the grounds offered for reasonable and trustworthy belief in our "basic" moral assumptions.

Before considering some of the objections that may be (and have been) urged against Dewey's conception of philosophy, I wish briefly to compare it with the conception of philosophy which has recently been popularized by contemporary logical empiricism. According to this school of thought, all human utterances, except statements of mathematics and logic, fall into two classes: utterances which, as signs or effects, express something about the persons making them; and utterances which represent in a symbolic way that some state of affairs is so or is not. Statements of the first class are neither true nor false, for they assert nothing. Statements of the second class may be true or false; they are meaningful because verifiable. The second class includes all of the propositions of the empirical sciences—natural and social. What about philosophical statements? Or, more accurately, statements made by philosophers which are grammatically correct but are not clearly either representative (empirical) statements or expressive ones. Such statements have been conventionally classified as falling into three groups: metaphysical (including ontology, epistemology, and normative ethics), psychological, and logical. Most logical empiricists assert that all the statements in the first group are expressive and therefore strictly meaningless; all the statements of the second group belong to the field of empirical science (except "rational psychology" and "intuitive psychology," which are part of metaphysics). This leaves logical analysis which constitutes the sole subject matter of philosophy.

Now in one sense Dewey, too, believes that philosophy may be defined as logical analysis. But his conception of logical analysis, as we shall see later, is not restricted to logical syntax, i.e., the formal rules which determine what constitutes a sentence and how given sentences may be transformed into others, but includes an analysis of the methods of general inquiry valid in all fields. And among these fields is one made up of statements which some logical empiricists, at least, have ruled out as purely expressive, viz., statements that assert that some value, belief, policy, assumption, or method is "better" or "worse" than others. Since every theoretical discipline, including logic, when confronted by a series of problems to be solved, does choose some assumption or method as better for its purpose than others, and since every art like medicine, law, etc., likewise engages in evaluation, we have a field which touches at some point every domain of thought and practice. Philosophers, according to Dewey, have always been concerned with these basic problems of reasonable or trustworthy belief—sometimes critically, sometimes not. His proposal to philosophers is that they continue with such concerns, in any field in which they have some mastery of the subject matter, in a self-conscious "scientific" way. Some, but not all, logical empiricists believe that such a proposal opens the doors to a revival of metaphysics, for no human action, they assert, where a basic choice is at issue, can ever be scientifically grounded.

There is, therefore, a correlated difference in the approach of Dewey and the main branch of the logical

empiricists to the history of philosophy. Long before
the logical empiricists, Dewey had shown that most of
the traditional problems of philosophy were pseudo
problems, i.e., they could not be solved even in their
own terms. In a much more formal way the logical empiricists did the same thing and stopped. But instead
of stopping with the demonstration of the logical futility of continuing the controversy over formulations
which in principle could never be adequate to any concrete problems, Dewey went on to inquire what the
genuine conflicts were which lay at the bottom of fruitless verbal disputes. If metaphysics is meaningless, why
should it be endowed by hard-headed governments? If
normative propositions are nonsensical, why should
people fight over them? Why should one variety of
nonsense be supported by one group and another variety by a different one? Dewey believes that philosophical analysis can illumine the apparent conflict over
meaningless sentences by showing how it grows out of
genuine conflicts in interest and evaluation. Just as
there is a "method behind madness" so there is a "meaning behind nonsense." Dewey's hypothesis is that even
in a crazy patchwork quilt of metaphysics, particularly
if it wins acceptance, we can find some response to the
same difficulties and predicaments of life which are at
the basis of political, cultural, and social struggles.
Dewey proposes that, without abandoning its critical
detachment, philosophy analyze these conflicts, put the
issues into focus by clarifying the ideas and ideals of
the contending parties, and suggest methods of dealing
with them which will make our choices "better" or more
intelligent.

Illustrations of this mode of approach to the problems of classical philosophy abound in Dewey's writings. He has thrown a flood of light on the generating attitudes responsible for much of ancient and modern philosophy. Where, for example, the logical empiricists see nothing but confused logical syntax in epistemological controversies over the priority of sensation or reason, subject or object, Dewey interprets the great systematic efforts to reduce one to another as an ever renewed struggle between two attitudes contending for exclusive mastery over social life—the radical and progressive on the one hand, the conservative and traditional on the other. When the specific problems of social change are faced, it is easy to see how necessary the roles of both sensation and reason are in initiating and controlling all changes that appeal to intelligence for acceptance.

We must now consider some of the chief types of objection which have been urged against Dewey's conception of philosophy. One of the commonest arguments against it is that it makes philosophy a handmaiden of narrow practice. It overlooks, so it is alleged, man's natural curiosity and sense of wonder before the mysteries of creation. It asks that philosophy, so to speak, pay for itself in specific utilities as if it were a business venture, forgetting that man's greatest glory expresses itself in conspicuously useless pursuits like pure mathematics, art, and other forms of play. This objection is based upon an obvious and almost willful misunderstanding. To begin with, when Dewey speaks of practice, he does not mean that philosophies must serve some immediate practical inter-

est but that if they have meaning they commit us to
some activity in relation to the world or situation which
calls it forth. This activity or practice may be evaluated as useful or useless, good or bad; but the crucial
question is whether such practice is relevant to the
problem with which the philosopher is concerned,
whether he is aware of its relevance, and is prepared
to accept the consequences as evidence for or against
the validity of his philosophy. It is sheer begging the
question to assume that philosophy is like pure mathematics and art. For these have a definite subject matter, problems, and procedures, whereas it is the very
nature of the subject matter of philosophy which is
in question. Chess may be useless, but we know what it
is about and can demonstrate propositions about possible moves. And surely it is not being claimed by
critics of Dewey's philosophy that if anything is useless it is therewith philosophical. To say that Dewey
would turn men away from wondering or blunt their
intellectual curiosity is as wrong as anything can be.
In fact that is part of his indictment of conventional
education. The tendency to wonder is as natural to
men as their breathing, but not so well developed, and
subject to many more frustrations. After all what does
it mean to wonder, to be *intellectually* curious? For
Dewey it means to fashion ideas, hypotheses, and their
alternatives, whose meaning and relevance depend upon
imaginative projection of their consequences for action
(practice, inquiry, research) of a specific kind in a
specific situation. That is the difference between intellectual wonder or vision, and daydreaming. When an
astronomer tells us he is wondering about the world,
we know what he is doing; but do we know what a

philosopher is doing when he wonders about the world? Does he?

Far from urging philosophers to restrict themselves to narrow factual surveys within the interstices of the special sciences as a way of establishing their usefulness, Dewey deplores the absence of speculative ideas. Philosophical inquiry should seek to make whatever inquiry is born of wonder not only rigorous but fruitful. He makes a plea, that would certainly sound strange coming from a worshiper of utility, for "the casting off of that intellectual timidity which hampers the wings of imagination, for speculative audacity, for more faith in ideas"—but in every case, the lead, meaning, and test of their ideas is to be found in a specific set of activities and practices related to concrete problems.

Further, if Dewey is right about the nature of philosophy, insofar as it is distinguishable from science, it is primarily an evaluation of evaluations in social and personal life. Whether we call such activity practical is not of importance. The self-styled practical man will not. But no matter what it is called, it is of momentous account because of its power to direct and redirect so many human practices. Philosophy, as well as other sciences, may have arisen out of wonder. But it is a wonder about what is most trustworthy or reasonable in the way of belief, and of life. That is why the philosophy a man has makes a difference, and will always make a difference, to the world. It would be true to say that for Dewey the impractical man is not he who has a theory or a philosophy but he who is unaware of the one he has and so cannot check or criticize what he is doing; while the practical man is not he who is busy just for the sake of being busy but who knows what he is doing and why.

The second type of criticism of Dewey's conception of philosophy takes him to task for neglecting the cosmic background of the human enterprise. Man and his day-by-day concerns, the objection runs, loom so large in Dewey's scheme of things that they blot out the eternal procession of the stars and the multiple-infinite vistas of a universe in comparison to which man is insignificant. One critic taxes him with having little consciousness of the loneliness of the individual soul adrift on uncharted seas of being. In striving to make the world a better place to live in, it is said, Dewey overlooks the fact that the world at its best is not worth much, that death, ugliness, and ignorance will always be the lot of man, that intelligence is weak compared to its rivals, and that the better part of wisdom is to resign ourselves to our fundamental limitations rather than to try to overcome them.

This type of criticism is based upon a glaring misreading of Dewey and a basic confusion of categories. Nowhere does Dewey suggest that even the widest use of intelligence will eliminate all human evils and imperfections. Indeed, it is the very imperfections of men as biological and social creatures, together with the precariousness of all existence, which constitute the matrix out of which all the problems that beset men arise. These problems can be met in various ways. One of them is by talking about the stars. The other is by bringing to bear all the resources of intelligence to increase the area of human and humane control, and, in a world where so much is frustrated by accidents that cannot be avoided, to reduce the number that can. How

many burdens under which men have needlessly suffered have been ascribed to the fixed character of the
cosmos, and therefore part of their eternal lot? Only
intelligence can distinguish in any given situation between what follows from the nature of things, and what
is due to human indifference and cruelty. Wisdom for
Dewey is not a weary resignation to human limitations. As if the basis of comparison could ever be the
romantic illusion of human beings free from all limitations! Wisdom is the unlamenting acceptance of whatever limitations intelligence discloses to be present in
the world, as the condition for increasing the role of
intelligence, beauty, and fellowship in experience.

The objection we are examining makes sense only
if it is legitimate to make an antithesis between the
meaning of human experience and the meaning of existence. For Dewey, it is meaningless to speak of the
meaning of existence. With critics of this variety in
mind, he writes: "It has become a cheap intellectual pastime to contrast the infinitesimal pettiness of man with
the vastnesses of the stellar universe. Yet all such com-
parisons are illicit. We cannot compare existence and
meaning; they are disparate. The characteristic life of
man is itself the meaning of vast stretches of existence,
and without it the latter have no meaning or existence.
There is no measure of physical existence and conscious experience because the latter is the only measure
there is for the former. The significance of being,
though not its existence, is the emotion it stirs, the
thought it sustains."

To put it another way, those who contrast the human foreground and the cosmic background in nature
forget that without reference to man there is no fore-

ground or background in nature at all. Men may prefer to follow the course of the stars rather than to work for the elimination of war and poverty. But it is a human preference and must be evaluated like all human preferences. There is nothing in Dewey's philosophy to forbid it. But he insists that if we are truly interested in broadening the scope of esthetic experience and intellectual adventure there are certain social conditions which must be fulfilled first.

A closer glance at this criticism "from the standpoint of eternity" shows that actually it is not a criticism of Dewey's conception of philosophy. It confirms it. For it does not deny that philosophy is concerned with a critical evaluation of values and beliefs; it only denies Dewey's specific evaluations. Its own allegiance, as a philosophy, is either to a certain "objective" theory of value or to a special set of values which it presumably believes it can establish as worthier than others. Its narrowness is revealed in the fact that it conceives of philosophy in such a way that answers to specific questions of what reasonable beliefs to hold are begged at the very outset. Those who contrast eternity with time, more often than not, are really contrasting past times with present times. A transcendent passion for "past times," Dewey once remarked, is "a form of pastime," legitimate enough if recognized as such but not obligatory upon everyone.

Chapter

III

THE NATURE OF IDEAS

A PHILOSOPHER is a man of ideas. He differs from other people who are concerned with ideas in that he has ideas about ideas. The easiest approach to a man's philosophy is usually through his theory of the nature of ideas, for many other aspects of his thought depend upon it. In the case of John Dewey, it would hardly be an exaggeration to say that almost all of the doctrines associated with his name can be inferred from his theory of the nature of ideas. For more than fifty years and in varied terminologies, he has been discussing ideas.

Dewey's interest in the nature of ideas is not hard to explain. Whatever else intelligence is, it is an affair of ideas. Concern with the origin, function, and tests of ideas is therefore inescapable on the part of anyone who believes in the methods of intelligence. We are living in a day where much is being said about plans and programs. But not all who glorify them can tell us what it means to have a plan, at what point it ceases being a slogan, how it differs from a fantasy, by what methods we determine whether plans have succeeded or failed. Without a clear understanding of what ideas are, it is impossible to answer questions of this kind.

Since no one else seems interested in making an analysis of ideas, the philosopher must do it. Philosophers have attempted to do it in the past, and every fresh analysis must do justice to their efforts, even if they turn out to have been misdirected. Part of the difficulty of the subject consists in picking one's way through the thicket of these different theories of ideas. There is no going around it, however, and even simplification has obvious limits. In Dewey's case the recompense is that his theory of ideas and the derivative notions of truth and validity light up his treatment of every major problem.

Of all the terms in the philosopher's vocabulary, "idea" is surely the most ambiguous. Not only in the philosopher's vocabulary. Ordinary speech shows many different senses of the term. It is used synonymously with words like perception, intent, guess, anticipation, form, function, presentation, image, to mention but a few. Only a careful attention to the context of the term, the situation within which it is used, and the action, symbolic or literal, by which it is controlled, enables us to determine in what sense the word idea is being employed.

No theory worth a second glance can account for all the different meanings of "idea." Nor can any theory of "ideas" be tested by its adequacy in accounting for the uses of the term unless we can distinguish in a workably clear way between these different meanings. Dewey's theory of ideas is a theory about "ideas" in the sense in which we say "knowledge is a process of getting ideas," "ideas are the life of mind," "have you an idea how this works?" In other words, Dewey is primarily interested in discovering the nature of "scientific" ideas, where science is broadly conceived to

cover every situation in which to have ideas is to make
a claim to have knowledge—good, bad, or indifferent.
If we are clear as to what ideas are in this sense, it
may turn out that some of the other senses are derivative. There is no reason why they should all be. But
the advantage of beginning in this way is that we can
control the adequacy of Dewey's hypothesis about ideas
by testing it in the light of what we can observe about
the life career of our own ideas in all situations where
having an idea and not having an idea correspond to
the distinction between claiming to have knowledge and
not making such a claim.

Most simply put, an idea, for Dewey, is a *plan of
action*. What kind of action? That depends upon the
situation in which the idea is formulated. Different ideas
in different fields involve different kinds of action. "It
may be chopping down a tree, finding a trail, or conducting a scientific research in mathematics, history, or
chemistry." But it is action of a physical kind that
involves the use of the body in a world of other bodies
and things. Since it is a plan of action, the idea presupposes the existence of something to be acted upon.
Ideas, therefore, never create what they act upon although a new creation may be the consequence of their
action. When there is no relevant specifiable difference
in the kind of actions that follow from entertaining
two ideas, the ideas are logically one and the same,
even though they sound different; when specifiable differences are observable, ideas are logically different,
even when they sound alike.

An idea is a *plan* of action. Like all other plans, it is
relevant to a problem. What kind of problem? Here
again the answer depends upon the particular difficul-

ties out of which problems arise and the particular purposes which are being frustrated by the difficulties. But an idea as a plan is directed to the future in a two-fold sense—to something to be done and to something expected from the doing. It is only as *plans* that "ideas are the promise of things hoped for, the symbol of things not seen."

A plan must meet certain conditions before it can succeed. But in meeting these conditions, as a form of action, it remakes or redoes these conditions in certain respects. To be intelligent is not merely, or even primarily, to be successful in achieving a certain end, for this may be a matter of luck. To be intelligent is to have a plan and to be able to distinguish it from other plans. The having of a plan means that we are able to indicate what specific operations must be performed in a specific milieu. It is often easier for others to tell whether or not we have a plan than for us. For they ultimately judge by what they observe while we may mistake a feeling of tension or elation for an idea, and tinkering for directed action.

This simple approach to ideas is not innocent. For as we shall see, it has significant implications, some apparently paradoxical, for the whole enterprise of scientific inquiry. Let us draw some of them and note how at every point they challenge some traditional or commonsensical assumption about the nature of ideas. First of all, if an idea is a plan of action, it is a property of organic *behavior*. To speak of ideas, then, as many philosophers have done, as if they have an existence, separate and apart from the body, is to be guilty of a contradiction in terms. Second, as a plan, an idea is a mode of response to a situation; *it is not a kind of stuff*—physical, mental, or neutral. To speak, then, of having ideas *in* one's head or *in* one's mind is a deceptive metaphor. Third, a planned response or behavior is a public action. Its very nature demands that it can be performed by others, at the very least observed by others. To speak, then, of ideas being private, a personal possession whose meaning cannot be shared or communicated, is illegitimate. These modes of speech taken literally generate insoluble problems with which philosophers have wrestled for centuries in vain.

Ideas conceived as plans of action have a constructive office in producing changes which mark the difference between unsettled and settled, problematic and resolved, situations. Such a conception runs counter to another view which admits that ideas have a function but insists this function is not to produce anything but "to reproduce" it correctly or accurately. It answers the question, What is it that we have ideas of? by saying that our ideas are *of* the physical world. But can an idea literally reproduce the physical world? No, but according to this view the qualities and relations of the physical world are reproducible or representable in ideas. What must an idea be, then, in order to be able to reproduce or represent the qualities of the things we have ideas of? The answers made indicate that ideas are believed to be of the nature of perceptions, lively or faint, or of images, clear or blurred, or of sensations, simple or compound.

It is true that the term "idea" is sometimes used in common discourse synonymously with perception, image, and sensation. What these are, in Dewey's view, we shall discuss in a subsequent chapter. But the question is whether this theory of the nature of ideas is adequate to explain the role of ideas in knowledge-getting contexts. Many philosophers have answered this question affirmatively; but, according to Dewey, such a position is disastrously wrong and, when consistently held, terminates in the belief that ideas, instead of being claims to knowledge, which like all other claims must be validated by certain techniques and operations, are themselves the sole objects of knowledge, and that therefore men are imprisoned in the magic circle of private, sensory experience.

Consider, then, as a test case for the validity of this theory of ideas, any idea which claims to be true or to lead to knowledge. How can it be identified with a sense quality or image of any kind? We stumble upon something and pick it up. We observe its color, feel its shape, smell its fragrance, and note as many qualities as we can. But we may list these qualities and still be compelled to ask: What is it? As qualities "they are the materials of problems." They themselves must be investigated and understood. The experience of these qualities is a natural event on all fours with other natural events. We can look a thing in the face all day and still not know what it is. Our knowledge begins when we can relate the qualities observed to their causes, when we can use them to make predictions, act on them to derive new qualities, show their functional dependence upon each other. Perceptions, images, and sensations are immediate; knowledge never is. As natural events, the former are strictly speaking neither true nor false. When noticed, they mark the point at which things break in upon the continuities of our behavior and provoke us to reflection, i.e., to formulate ideas which redirect behavior. The ideas may be true or false but not that which provokes us into forming them.

Sensations are the stimuli not the gateways to knowledge. They are necessary to knowledge not only as stimuli but as checks, controls, signs. But, if and when we are *agreed* that in a given case knowledge has been achieved, we can show that such knowledge is the consequence of our having common ideas, not common sensations. What does it mean to say that we have common sensations, anyhow, when on most theories of sensations they are private and incommunicable?

The identification of ideas with sensations, wherever ideas are recognized as "candidates for knowledge," was recognized as a mistake by many philosophers long before Dewey. Sensations are discrete; ideas have a pattern. Sensations are specific and unrepeatable; ideas are general, constant, and uniform. The ways in which sensations are organized, caused, related, are not themselves sensations. This was known to Plato, to Spinoza, to Kant. Ideas, for them, were the source of Reason, Order, Connection. They were not present in Sensations. They had to be found in Ideas. What were Ideas? Not plans of action but—and here we have divergence among the different schools of rationalism—Forms of Being, Intuitions, Categories of Transcendental Mind.

The converse of a mistake may be another mistake, particularly when it shares some of the assumptions of the original one. According to Dewey, all of these rationalistic theories of the nature of ideas, even when they admitted, as the Kantians did and the Platonists did not, that sensory experience was necessary to knowledge, were mistaken because their account of ideas was incompatible with the actual role of ideas in scientific inquiry—the field of pre-eminent knowledge.

According to the rationalist theory, the conclusion of any inquiry can be regarded as genuine knowledge only insofar as it can be identified with, or subsumed under, an Idea, Insight, or Form which is itself certain. Otherwise an infinite regress is set up. What is presented as knowledge can then pass muster only if it is demonstrable that at some point it is a logical or probable consequence of an Idea which is immediately and self-evidently true.

Yet no idea in science, whether as premise or conclusion, postulate or law, rule or description, is regarded as self-evident. Every idea must justify itself. The considerations offered in justification vary. But what they all have in common is this: reference to the consequences of their use and not to antecedent certainties. The validation of scientific ideas of any kind is always offered in terms of observable consequences "which satisfy the conditions set by the nature of the problem in hand." Any theory of ideas which entails the view that some ideas must be self-evidently true rules itself out of court because it rules out all scientific knowledge as genuine knowledge. And no sooner does it present the specific ideas which it regards as self-evident than it becomes apparent that they possess the alleged character of self-evidence only in the eyes of a few. There is irony in the fact that more universal agreement exists about scientific ideas that make no pretense of being self-evidently true than about any axioms or self-evident truths which have ever been advanced at any time by any philosophical school.

Another consequence of the view that Ideas as Forms

or Rational Intuitions are the sole intelligible criteria
of knowledge, is that the acquisition of *new* knowledge
as the outcome of processes of reflective inquiry becomes a mystery. All knowledge had to be identified
with the rational Forms, derived from Mind or Being,
or reduced to illustrations of such Forms. New knowledge was "explained" by assimilating it to Ideas
immediately grasped by Thought without the interven-
tion of observation or inference. Yet the whole history
of science shows that scientific inquiry makes progress
by continually bursting through the old and familiar
Forms of explanation. It sets up its own standards and
criteria of valid knowledge by accepting "the *consequences* of their experimental operations as constituting the known object," instead of "proving" that the
new knowledge won was identical with what was already
known.

The third consequence of traditional rationalism is
that all knowledge which seems to be a result of controlled experience turns out to be a case of recognition.
We can only know what in some sense we have already
known. This is the Platonic answer to the puzzle of
how a person who is ignorant can ever learn anything,
for he must not only know enough to ask a question
but to recognize the answer as the right one when it is
given. But once we see that ideas in science are presented as hypotheses and not as transcripts of Forms
of Being; once we relate ideas to the operations they
elicit and the differences in things which result from
such operations; once we see that whatever knowledge
we bring to a new inquiry both tests and is tested in
that inquiry—all the puzzles disappear. Cognition no
longer pretends to be mere recognition but a mode of

intelligent action of the organism as a whole in solving its problems.

We can now list some of the advantages of Dewey's theory of ideas as plans of action. It liberates us from the desperate expedient of ruling out science as knowledge, and from the myth that we can only know what we have once forgotten. It saves us from the dubious psychology and worse philosophy that seeing, hearing, and feeling are not merely believing but knowing. But these are only negative virtues of the theory. It explains by positive evidence observable features of the actual use of ideas in inquiry. It explains what has been a great mystery to all other theories of ideas, viz., how thinking can affect things, how thought can be practical, and why its presence or absence makes a concrete difference to the world. Every other theory fails at this point, for it makes ideas either useless, or reduplicative, or the source of the very things they affect. Dewey's theory avoids these blind alleys in its explanation of the functional roles of sensory experience, accumulated knowledge, and hypotheses in all inquiry. And, finally, by showing that an idea is an acting out of a plan, controlled by some features of the objective situation and controlling others, it explains the "creative" power of ideas. Properly interpreted, ideas are never almighty but always efficacious. Whoever claims to have an idea, and not an image, or biological spasm, or ineffable vision, presents the world with "tools to search for materials to solve a problem."

From this primary theory of the nature of ideas, Dewey is able to show that two other usages of the term are derivative. In the behavior which exhibits a plan of action, i.e., in the behavior which enables us to recognize that an idea is at work, "ideas" are used, where the term "ideas" is interchangeable with "meanings," "conceptions," "abstractions." It is also observed that in inquiry things are used which are referred to as "meaningful," "significant," or "signs." How are these two senses of the term "idea" related to the one discussed in the previous section? We shall discuss them in reverse order.

A perplexing situation arises. What can be the matter? The answers suggested are ideas whose meanings are disclosed in the respective methods of inquiry to which they lead. Here to have an idea is to have a meaning, and to have a meaning is to have an idea, and both are properties of behavior. This is the primary sense of idea or meaning. But in carrying out our inquiry, certain things rather than others are considered relevant, certain data are attended to and others ignored. These things and data are *meaningful* and are directly used in the process of inquiry without having to show their credentials. This is the test tube, that is a poison, this other a warning sound of a discharge. If these things were not meaningful, inquiry would be stopped short. We could not distinguish one plan of action from another, not to speak of carrying it out. In all inquiry not only are some things already meaningful but some other things become meaningful as a result of what we discover.

Now how can *things* be meaningful or become meaningful, particularly if we believe that the primary sense of meaning qualifies *human* behavior? And the answer is that unless things become elements of the pattern of

inquiry-behavior, or have once been elements of previous patterns, it is nonsense to say that they are meaningful. But in virtue of what relation or status within
inquiry-behavior do things become meaningful? In virtue of their usability as *means* to achieve certain consequences, or in virtue of the fact that they express
consequences the means to which must be discovered.
The things already assumed to be meaningful in any
present inquiry have proved to be instrumentally efficacious in previous inquiries. That is why *they* are
used in present inquiry and not others. The things
which establish themselves as meaningful do so only because they are "means to" some consequence. Things
derive meaning and take on added meaning only as a
result of inquiry. These meanings are as "objective"
as you please but they are acquired in and through inquiry, i.e., insofar as they enter into some actual or
possible means—consequence relation. Outside of discourse or inquiry things have no meaning. But discourse and inquiry never begin *de novo*. That is why in
any given situation most things already have significance, but taken together they do not add up.

There remains the sense of meaning or idea in which
it is used synonymously with "abstract" idea or "general" conception. In the course of establishing the
meaning of things, a stock of already-fixed meanings is
used. These meanings, themselves "taken to be secure
and warranted," enter into plans of action to identify
things and interpret results. Every common noun is
such a standardized meaning. Sometimes they do not
seem to have any reference to things, directly or indirectly, and generate problems about which we shall
have something to say later. But they are indispensable

if inquiry is to proceed or ever reach a fruition. For Dewey, these conceptions have crystallized out of myriads of previous plans of action. Where they are unambiguous, they epitomize a definite set of habits that can be brought into play without further reflection, until or unless their application strikes a snag. They are like ready-made tools which are used to fashion other tools that in turn achieve some specific purpose. Because they generalize and standardize the knowledge won in a whole class of previous cases, they furnish ready-made patterns for possible use in any fresh inquiry, thus introducing an enormous economy into thinking behavior.

The three main instrumental functions of abstract meanings or conceptions in inquiry are listed by Dewey as (a) identifying something unknown by describing it in terms of some familiar character, kind, or quality; (b) supplementing knowledge by extending the scope of possible observation, i.e., if what is observed is identified as having a character, then we can expect to make certain future observations in virtue of what that character entails; (c) ordering whatever knowledge we have by making the systematic nexus of things clear in the light of a system of meanings.

Here is something which we have found clinging to the trunk of a tree. Is it a metal, or a plant, or an animal? It is identified, say, as an animal. Whatever is known about animals is forthwith assumed to hold for the object identified. In this way our information is immediately supplemented by the possession of all the known qualities and characters that anything which is an animal must have. The meaning of animal is not isolated but is related to a whole system of meanings

whose study is the science of biology. The thing identified as an animal is incorporated as a part of the whole
kingdom of living things related to and differentiated
from plants on the one hand and inanimate things on
the other.

Concluding this phase of the discussion, we may
say that meaning or idea has three different but related senses. Meaning is primarily a property of behavior. Meaning is secondarily a property of things
used, revised, or constructed in the course of that
behavior. Meaning is thirdly a set of previously built-up
habits automatically brought into play in carrying inquiry to completion.

Perhaps the most difficult point to grasp is Dewey's
doctrine that "abstract meanings," the third sense of
"idea," express customary habits of action. Many philosophers believe that abstract ideas or concepts are
derived differently. In the interest of clarity we will
state and contrast with Dewey's views two of the most
influential theories of the origin of conceptions (universals, essences). One view asserts that these "ideas"
arise as a result of the comparison of various members
of a class or kind in the course of which all points of
difference are dropped until what remains is the common quality or set of qualities shared by all. This last
gives us the meaning or concept. Thus, by inspecting
a collection of variously colored and sized horses and
attending to the characters they have in common, we
derive the "idea" (meaning, concept) of equinity or
horsiness.

A moment's thought will show that this view is unten-
able. For the comparison is here being made between
various members of a class or kind which is assumed al-

ready to have meaning. We compare Sorrell and Dobbin and Seabiscuit to get the core of meaning "equinity"; we do not compare any of them with the Empire State Building or the Kohinoor diamond. Why? Because we already know that Sorrell and Dobbin and Seabiscuit are horses. That is to say, we already have to know the meaning of equinity in order to round up the various animals to be compared with each other. This whole view of abstraction is therefore circular and question-begging on its face. For Dewey, a concept is developed by transferring the response originally made to an object of definite traits used for a certain purpose in a situation, to other objects which seem to function the same way in similar situations. We expect anything which reveals the "defining" trait in question to behave in the same way as the first object that has been named "horse," and if it does not, we revise our initial meaning of horse, i.e., we look for some other "defining" trait which will enable us to handle new things in a way to get the same results as in the old. A child will at first call any large, four-legged animal a "horsie" until he fails to observe the familiar behavior associated with this trait.

Conceptions become general and fixed by "use and application," not by cancelling out the properties of an aggregate of things until we reach some least common denominator. That which defines an object is not a particular trait which a certain given number of objects must possess, but that which enables us to make the greatest number of reliable predictions about what consequences to expect when it is present or absent. When anything is assigned a meaning, some trait of the thing is regarded as a sign that some other traits are expected. The meaning is an indication to act in a certain way. Only by a figure of speech is the meaning *in* the thing. What makes a piece of wood a pawn or king in a chess game is not any natural quality it possesses but a rule as to how it can be moved. The natural quality is meaningful when it becomes a sign that the rule can be applied to it. Similarly, abstract meanings tell us what operations are to be performed on things (or symbols) in any given situation. They express common habits of action and expectation.

There is another theory of abstraction which grants with Dewey that, strictly speaking, meanings, ideas, and concepts are not *in* things. Things may suggest meanings but they do not contain them. It also grants with Dewey that meanings are not *in* the mind; they are not sensations, images, or emotions. What, then, are meanings? The answer takes them out of the world altogether. Because they are neither physical nor psychical, they are regarded as metaphysical, "self-subsistent essences," which are beheld or discovered by the mind and are not generated in the process of human association. The difficulties in this view are legion, but they all flow from neglecting the function of meanings in inquiry and discourse and failing to observe that the only way we can tell whether anyone *is* beholding an essence and *what* he is beholding, is by the differential consequences in action which result therefrom. There are many things which arise in the course of human experience which are neither physical nor psychical and yet which we would not class as metaphysical, for example, a franchise, a government post, a declaration of love or hate. A meaning as an organizing plan of action is as objective as anything you please. It is not simply

physical or psychical although it has physical and
psychical consequences. There is no need, therefore, to
hypostatize meanings into superstatic and transempiri-
cal entities. There is no observable quality possessed
by meanings which renders their dislocation from the
context of human inquiry necessary.

To say that meanings are objective is another way of
saying that they can be communicated. And communication, whether it be by sounds, symbols, or gestures is
a social activity. It is in the processes of social behavior, then, that meanings are born. The connection
between language, as the use of symbols, and meaning
is intrinsic. Language does not carry or transmit ideas
or meanings that have status antecedently and independently of it. Language is a mode of interaction and
association between at least two people. "It presupposes an organized group to which these creatures belong, and from whom they have acquired their habits
of speech." Whatever is true of language, is true of
meaning. If one is the condition for the presence of
mind or intelligence, so is the other. Language is a
means of establishing co-operation and congruent behavior between men, of sharing experience by leading
to activities that function together in modifying some
aspect of their common world. Ideas and meanings are
forged and stabilized in this process of adapting the
behavior of human beings to each other and the world
in which they live. The objectivity of meanings lies in
their communicability. But communication is not a
process in which anything physical or psychical is
transmitted. What we call the leap of understanding
in communication is an anticipation of what is to come,
not a passive absorption of thing or thought. "To un-

derstand is to anticipate together, is to make a cross reference which, when acted upon, brings about a partaking in a common, inclusive undertaking." To realize that the social process is the matrix of all meanings is to abandon forever all theories which assign to meanings a supernatural status.

There are several objections to Dewey's theory of ideas which must be considered in order to fill out this exposition and give a proper emphasis to two central features. Some preliminary remarks are necessary to bring out the force of the objections.

In ordinary speech, whenever we attribute a quality to an object, we are aware of the fact that it is only because the object has some relation to other objects (things, people, light, instruments, etc.) that the specific quality in question is present. A hat has this particular shade of blue only in this light. Wax may be molded when it is brought near some source of heat. Shrimps are nourishing only to certain kinds of digestive systems. Qualities, then, are effects of an interaction between two or more things whose "original" properties in turn depend upon other relationships and interactions. To experience things, according to Dewey, is to act on them (not create them) in some way. *What* is experienced is the result of an interaction in which the behavior of the body is an integral part. Things experienced are as much an outcome of interacting processes, but not in the same way, as things burned, broken, or beautified. That is to say, they are to some extent modified in the reciprocal influences that develop in the course of the interaction. These modifications are as much a part of the nature of things as the "original properties," which, as we have seen, are likewise dependent upon other types of interaction. Anything may be experienced, i.e., taken or acted upon, in different ways. A thing loved, a thing eaten, a thing known, involve different ways of proceeding in respect to it and different consequences of such proceeding. For Dewey, one type of experience is distinguished from the other only in terms of these objective procedures and consequences. But no matter how a thing is experienced, something happens to it as a result of the processes of behavior into which it is introduced. When we speak of the powers it possesses "antecedent" to the experience, this is an inference based upon the qualities it reveals in experience. The "nature" of a thing is not locked up by, for, and in itself but, like anything that has a career in time, acquires new properties as a result of the manifold ways in which the organism acts upon it.

That things are modified in some respect when they become elements of an interacting whole is a commonplace. It is illustrated in events as different as the birth of a pearl in an oyster and the emergence of a sausage from a machine. But that things are modified when they enter into a behavior pattern of knowledge-getting seems to be a monstrous paradox. For—so runs the objection—if knowing makes a difference to that which is known, how can we ever truly know what the thing is? Is not Dewey opening the door wide to idealism, subjectivism, and all the other self-defeating isms which he himself has so effectively exposed? The function of knowledge, it is objected, is to report what is the case, not to transform it. If thinking is a process in which "the object of knowledge" is altered, then it can result only in error. If an idea of anything is a plan of action which changes that of which it is an idea, how can we ever form an adequate idea?

The objection, however, turns upon an ambiguity in the phrase, "object of knowledge." It owes its verbal plausibility to a shift between two distinct senses of the phrase and a misremembering of Dewey's insistence that in any concrete situation ideas are candidates for knowledge. "Object of knowledge" may refer either to the situation or thing which provokes inquiry, which makes us ask: What is this? or it may refer to the outcome or resultant effect of inquiry, i.e., to the answer to the question. For Dewey, the change takes place in the situation which provokes inquiry, in the things that are involved in the situation and which are modified by the behavior of hands, feet, instruments, or whatever else we relevantly use in acting out or testing our "ideas." No change takes place in the outcome of inquiry. The outcome of inquiry is the "object of knowledge." The idea is the anticipation or prediction that the outcome of the inquiry will be one thing rather than another. It directs the inquiry; and, when it does so successfully, it is recognized as adequate, as having realized its original promise.

Knowledge is achieved when we discover what is the case. But to discover what is the case something must be done, even if it is nothing more than a controlled looking or hearing from a new perspective. The doing does not change what we discover. That would be madness. It changes or rearranges the situation which provoked the inquiry in order to determine what is the case. What is the case (or "object of knowledge") is always something *to be* discovered. If it were given, there would be no need to look for it. Inference results in knowledge when, on the basis of some actual or possible transformation of the situation which challenges thought, we can predict what will be the case. Our preliminary ideas of what is the case offer themselves to be tested. They are not mental photographs or carbon copies of things. If they were, they would be useless to the precise degree that they were faithful, since they would reflect those very features in the original situation that were puzzling. They are guiding principles which indicate how to act in the situation to make it less puzzling.

The second objection asserts that Dewey's behavioristic theory of ideas (or knowing) is guilty of the same "reduction" of thought to speech, and of speech to laryngeal movements of the throat, as the behavioristic theory of J. B. Watson. It therefore shares all the difficulties of the latter. This is not so much an objection as a misunderstanding, and some words are in order on the relation between Dewey and Watson. As one of the founders of the functional school of psychology out of which Watson developed, Dewey challenged the view that "consciousness" is both a special kind of subject matter and an organ of immediate apprehension of its own contents. This is common to both. But Dewey's concept of behavior, especially thinking behavior, is quite different from that of Watson's. Although he does not reach conclusions that violate common sense and common usage, his behaviorism is more thoroughgoing than that of Watson and his school.

According to Watson, thought in the form of speech is a biological reaction to a stimulus. The stimulus is something which is received by the senses. Speech recognizes or expresses what is received; it does nothing to the stimulus or the situation of which the stimulus is a part. As thought, speech behavior does not modify or direct the activity of inquiry, on Watson's view. It is already complete when the verbal response occurs. The response is not a quest for the meaning of the stimulus. It repeats in language the meaning that the stimulus is supposed to have. In Dewey's terms, Watson assumes that the stimulus is itself the object of knowledge rather than a challenge to discover through further activity what the object of knowledge is. For Watson, speech or thought "is a futile echoing" of what is already known when the stimulus is given.

Dewey is emphatic in asserting that "the identification of knowing and thinking with speech is wholly in the right direction." But not all speech is a mode of knowing or thinking, not to mention sighs, cries, and groans which are also laryngeal movements. The speech which is thought (ideas) evokes a behavior of the entire organism, certainly much more than the vocal organs and their adjoining parts, to a situation which is problematic, not known. By identifying stimulus with object of knowledge, and laryngeal reactions with thought, Watson shows that he is wedded to the belief in immediate knowledge. According to Dewey, he also shows that he misunderstands the nature of speech.

Speech, to be sure, is a form of laryngeal movement. But as thought, it is not only that. It is originally a way of making a responsive adjustment to the activities of some other person, and secondarily a direction to ourselves to co-ordinate our behavior with the anticipated behavior of someone else. It is primarily social rather than biological. We can only soliloquize because we have already conversed. The upshot of meaningful speech is to achieve a coherent system of behavior among different observers (auditors and speakers) in relation to a common problem or difficulty. We may consider such achievement as confirmation or knowledge of the same object. It is as legitimate to speak of consciousness, mind, awareness, as it is of breathing, digesting, running, provided we can indicate the differential acts and consequences of (symbolic) behavior by which we note their presence or absence.

Chapter

IV

TRUTH

G IVEN a theory of ideas, it is not hard to predict what theory of truth will be drawn from it. For truth or falsity is a property of ideas. Failure to realize this results in confusion. As existences, things are neither true nor false; nor are mental states, whatever they are. What we meaningfully *say* about them is true or false. The saying, for Dewey, is also a direction for doing. It is the consequences of what is done, therefore, which determines whether the saying is true or false.

How shall we go about testing theories of truth? The simplest way is to ask how specific truths come to be established in inquiry, and to note what guides us in accepting this statement purporting to be true rather than some other statement in this particular situation. There is much more agreement as to what are truths than about theories of truth. Indeed, Dewey insists that his theory is a theory of truths—truths of the common garden variety and not of anything that can be called The Truth. In what contexts are judgments accepted as true? What functional role do propositions play in inquiry which ends in truth or certified knowledge? The answers to these questions must be found in any adequate theory of truth.

If an idea is a plan of action, it is clear that it arises to solve a recognized difficulty in whatever it is we are doing. Ideas are *plans* of action because they suggest themselves as problem solvers, no matter what kind of problem is involved. Of two plans of action, that one is accepted as true, which is "better," "more satisfactory," or "more successful" for the problem in hand. Were we speaking of tools or instruments, no one would object to the words which we have put in quotation marks. But when we speak of ideas, there are many who find such words disgracefully inappropriate because they seem to connote something private or capricious. Now, as a matter of fact, when we say that this diagnosis is "better" or "more successful" than that, no one would dream of suggesting that our statement is an expression of arbitrary preference because it is obvious that a patient, a method of operation, and a set of observable traits serve as controls. It is in reference to them and not to our own wishes and hopes that we call the diagnosis "better" or "more successful." However, when ideas are adjudged true because they are "better" or "more satisfactory," all reference to the objective problem is suppressed by those who profess to see in Dewey's use of these terms subjective intentions.

For Dewey, any theory which leads to the conclusion that there are private truths thereby discloses its inadequacy. For truths are what people look to in order to find guide and anchorage in the tumultuous seas of opinion. Problems are settled and stay settled only when common agreement has been secured by the use of a common method of inquiry. In order to make this point as emphatic as possible and to distinguish it from some other loosely formulated doctrines which are embraced by the generic term "pragmatism," Dewey has stressed the fact that "the success," "the satisfactori-

ness" of a plan of action is to be defined exclusively in
terms of predicted consequences. In other words, an
idea is true if, as a result of acting it out—an experiment—we are able to verify certain specifiable consequences of believing it. Note, not any old consequence
which may give us personal satisfaction but consequences that are anticipated in virtue of the specific
plan to be followed and which in certain situations may
be far from pleasant.

My throat is parched, and I look around for water
to quench my thirst. I take a sip out of a glass and get
a taste of bitter almonds. I suspect that the water may
have been poisoned. If it is a poison, then, were I to
administer it to some living things, certain things would
result. I may be the only living thing around and,
wisely or unwisely, decide to test the water out on my-
self. The last thing in the world I may be able to say
as a result is "Yes, the water is poisoned." The consequences would be quite satisfactory in enabling me to
solve the problem of whether the water is poisoned or
not (provided I have no evidence that anything else in
the environment or in the state of my organism accounts for the observed consequences of drinking the
water); but, unless I were intent upon committing
suicide, this would be the only thing satisfactory about
the consequences. Yet it would be enough; every other
reference would be irrelevant.

This and only this theory of truths does Dewey call
pragmatism. In more technical language: "All judgments of fact have reference to a determination of
courses of action to be tried and to the discovery of
means for their realization ... all propositions which
state discoveries and ascertainments would be hypo-

thetical, and their truth would coincide with their tested consequences effected by intelligent action. This theory may be called pragmatism." What has this to do with subjectivism, impressionism, or wishful and willful believing?

But, someone is sure to ask, is there not something in the nature of things, is there not some "objective reality," to which an idea must "correspond" or with which it must "agree" before we can regard it as true? And if there is, must we not admit that certain "real things" authenticate truths which are absolutely valid antecedent to any inquiry? Must we not know what is "real" before we know what is true? And is there not a justified verbal usage which speaks directly of things as true, such as a true portrait, a true blade, a true sign?

Such modes of speech are harmless provided we recognize that the terms "correspond" and "agree" have different meanings depending upon the type of things which are said to correspond or agree. For example, when we say that the size or the cut of the carpet "corresponds" with the floor, we mean that we can lay the carpet so that its borders are physically superposed to make a snug fit at every point where the floor meets the walls of the room. When we say that a theatergoer's ticket "agrees" with the number of the seat he occupies, we mean that the numeral on a pasteboard is the same as the numeral on the back or side of his seat. Now, if an idea is a plan of action, it obviously becomes impossible to speak of correspondence or agreement in the above senses. But if an idea is assumed to be something else—a psychic substance, a neural spark, an image, or an intuited meaning—the

above notion of correspondence or agreement (and
many others which we have no space to consider here)
is every whit as inapplicable. Can an idea, presumably
a psychic entity, ever be superimposed on a floor in the
same way as a carpet? Can an idea ever agree with an
object in the same way as two numerals agree? An
idea of a number is not a numeral nor can it ever be
inspected in the way pasteboards and seats are. Ideas
"correspond" with things in a way in which no other
things do. They do not duplicate or mirror things. Indeed, what would be the point of having them if they
did? They correspond or agree with things only in the
sense that they lead to something expected as a result
of action. Their degree of correspondence is measured
by their degree of reliability.

   To be sure we do sometimes speak of true or real
Indians, diamonds, and maps, and of false or counterfeit bills, counts, and antiques. But whenever a thing is
called true or real, it is the result of some judgment
about it, some way of acting toward it, which has established itself as reliable or trustworthy; and whenever a
thing is called false or counterfeit, it is because the
judgments made about it and the behavior which results from the judgment, lead to a fiasco, a frustration
of logical expectations. If we knew the precise degree
of reliability or unreliability that attaches to any statement that had meaning, we would know all that could
be known about things. A "true" map—and ideas have
often been compared to maps—is not one which depends upon a literal reproduction of the physical features and relations in the object mapped, for many
different kinds of maps can be drawn from the same ter-
rain. "Any map in any system is 'true' (that is, valid)

if its operational use produces the consequences that
are intended to be served by the map."

The truth or adequacy of an idea, then, depends upon
whether the predictions made about the consequences of
acting on it are verified. But it may be objected that the
consequences of any judgment of fact are infinite
whereas the consequences which are actually verified are
finite, so that no judgment can claim to be true. The
objection would be unanswerable if *all* the consequences
of an idea had to be verified before it can be declared
true. It would be an objection not only to the experimental theory of truth but to every other theory. Actually, however, all the consequences of an idea do not
have to be verified before we can call the idea "true." If
we take into account the problematic context in which
the idea arises, then we can see that only those consequences are relevant which bear upon the resolution of
the difficulty.

We meet an individual and wonder whether he is as
skillful in his art as he professes to be. We test our
hypothesis about his capacity by observing the things
he does. Whether one or two or a hundred observations
are necessary to reach a conclusion depends upon the
class of situations of which this particular situation is
a member. What number of observations is sufficient as
a test of the truth of an idea is a function of the problem, and the history of human effort in dealing with
similar problems. Here no theory of truth can decide
but only the working habits and conventions of the
scientific workers themselves. These may vary from field
to field. Even in some one field different types of problems are recognized which demand a different number and
kinds of observations before the conditions for making

a judgment are satisfied. That is why many scientists themselves rarely speak of a theory or a hypothesis as "true" but as "more adequate," "better," or "more satisfactory" for settling the problem in hand.

If the relation of ideas to problems is lost sight of, many puzzles about the nature of verification arise. The idea is tested by observed consequences; but, when these are isolated from their effect upon the initial problem, the question is sure to arise: Why are *these* observations decisive? Since we cannot assume that any statement about any observation is necessarily true, why do we not go on to test that statement? And if we do, we can still ask the same questions that we have raised about the previous statements, and so on. But once we recall that the observation is the result of something tried, something done, then it is not so much a question of the consistency between the verbal form of the observation statement and the verbal form of the idea but rather a question of the practical bearing of the observation on the elimination of the difficulties in the original problem.

If truth or falsity is a property which an idea takes on as a result of its career in action, then it follows that there are no immediately true propositions. But does not such a conclusion do violence to the belief of some people that there are immediately true propositions? It does. The problem, then, is to determine whether there are any immediately true propositions, and, if there are none, why it is that we sometimes speak as if there were.

Propositions are sometimes regarded as immediately true because they are immediately *used* in a particular inquiry. A corpse is found at the base of a building.

Is it an accident, suicide, or murder? In the course of even the simplest inquiry, many propositions are assumed to be true. They function as instruments of preparing data which serve to test hypotheses. There is no doubt that psychologically we have no hesitation in employing them in particular situations. Unless there were some things which we knew already, we could never get started on anything new. It is immediacy of use which accounts for the impression of immediacy of validity. Validity, however, is determined by fruits and consequences. Successful use bestows preferment and privilege but not in perpetuity. At any definite time, what was immediately taken to be true or adequate may fail to prove itself. It may have to be qualified. It may have to be abandoned. After a sufficient number of successful applications in use, a proposition may pass as empirically warranted. We may never even entertain doubts about it. But absolutely guaranteed it cannot be. Nor is it reasonable to demand absolute guarantees.

The second class of ideas or propositions which seem to be immediately true are those taken to confirm a hypothesis. If the evidence leads us to believe that the man whose fingerprints are found on the cigarette lighter, so dexterously used as the lethal weapon, is the murderer, then, when we observe the prints of Mr. X, we can tell at a glance whether the first set is his. What is it that "we can tell at a glance" here? Certainly not that Mr. X is the murderer. That depends upon all sorts of assumptions which are theoretically questionable, e.g., that no two people can have the same prints. But, it might be said, what we can tell at a glance, and tell infallibly, unless we are lying, is that

the prints of Mr. X have such and such a character. I
may make a mistaken inference about the significance
or ownership of these prints before me, but I cannot
possibly be mistaken about what I see. Do we not in
fact have direct, immediate, and infallible knowledge of
all sense data without resorting to any other past or
future experience? Have we not here something more
than what is empirically warranted? Something absolutely guaranteed?

On Dewey's theory of truth the answer is no. Statements which describe what we observe may be vague,
incomplete, even erroneous. Psychologically, the seeing of something, and the describing in words of what
is seen, are two different acts. Not everyone is able to
"tell what he sees" about what lies in his direct field of
vision. The trained observer makes fewer errors, not
only in mediate interpretation but in "immediate" report. And a report of what is seen is not as immediate
as we think. An element of memory enters into the
description of what we have seen, and memory may be
vague, confused, and mistaken.

More important is the realization that a statement
about an observation acquires significance in any inquiry only insofar as it asserts something which other
people can verify, too. Suppose, for the sake of the
argument, it were true that I could not possibly be
mistaken about what *I* observe. My neighbors and scientific coworkers cannot observe what I observe if the
latter is a unique, private occurrence, which on this
theory it must be. Nor can I observe what they are
observing if observation is immediate and infallible.
But we can observe each other's physical and verbal
behavior. The observation statement is a form of be-

havior which acquires significance in inquiry only insofar as it is congruent with the behavior patterns of other observers. Nor is it a matter of the coherence of statements with each other when they are isolated from the specific practice with which such statements are customarily associated. Two people may say: "The room is warm"; but if, under certain conditions, as a result of their statement, they do diametrically opposite things, we are justified in inferring that they have made different reports of what is the case. Two people may utter statements that are formally contradictory, but if they proceed to act in the same way in relation to the difficulty which gave rise to an inquiry, they are taken to have made the same report. It is always possible in principle to tell whether behavior is congruent and to test both the coherence and validity of observation statements in terms of such congruence. It is impossible in principle to compare what is directly experienced by different individuals if it is assumed that they cannot be mistaken when they honestly report what they have experienced. It is impossible in principle for any observer to communicate the difference between the two observations "I see red" and "I see green," without relating these statements to specifically different consequences which flow from their assertion.

If the truth of an idea is determined by the future consequences of acting upon it, how shall we account for true ideas about the past? For the past is something which seems to be over and done with. "Cornwallis surrendered to Washington at Yorktown." If we grant that this proposition is true, the reference seems to be to an event not now present, to a unique and therefore unrepeatable occurrence more than a hundred

years ago. The truth of the proposition does not seem
to depend upon anything observable in the present or
future but solely upon whether the event referred to
actually took place in the past. But, once we make a
few necessary distinctions, it will be clear that this is
not the case, and that the truth of propositions about
the past are exactly of the same logical form as propositions about anything else.

To begin with, let us suppose that we are talking
about something which occurred in the past but which
has no existential or historical connection with anything observable in the present or future, say like the
adventures of the first group of men who crossed the
Atlantic. (Assuming that Columbus and his group were
not the first.) Could any statement about them be anything more than a part of a legend or some fictional
invention designed for an artistic purpose? Indeed, if
there were no connection with anything that followed,
why should we say that these were the first to cross?
Or that their adventures took one form rather than
another? Let us now look at the statement made about
Cornwallis. In what way does it differ from legends
about the first seafarers? Obviously in this: that certain evidence is at hand which enables us to verify it.
But to say that this evidence is at hand is to say that
certain continuities can be established—both of records and events—from the surrender of Cornwallis
down to the present. This continuity is found in the
varied series of consequences which followed the surrender. When it is asserted that "Cornwallis surrendered," what is meant is that if something is done to
test the assertion the series of consequences of Cornwallis' surrender will be found to run into the future,

and that only insofar as these future consequences can be confirmed are we justified in maintaining that the original proposition is true.

Note this does not mean that there are no such things as past events; or that yesterday's occurrence would not have taken place unless today's occurrence had materialized; or that knowledge about the past is impossible. What we are trying to determine is precisely what it means to have knowledge about the past. There may very well have been seafarers across the Atlantic who disappeared without leaving a trace. The occurrence of an event does not necessarily lead to our having knowledge about it. To have knowledge about the occurrence means that some of its effects are *now* observable, and that the test of the truth of a proposition about the past is the character of its present or future effects. The past becomes an object of knowledge only when we can tell of what present or future it is the past. Otherwise how distinguish between two past events, how determine whether or not an event ever was a *past* event, how in any specific case differentiate between an actual *event* and a fairy tale?

If we verify a judgment about a past event by its effects or consequences in the present and future, and if we verify a judgment about a present event in the same way, what is the difference between past and present events? The difference would lie in the fact that past and present events have different kinds of present and future effects.

The flavor of paradox disappears if we bear in mind that, for Dewey, memory judgments and judgments about the historical past are logically of the same form. Suppose someone says that he remembers an occurrence during his first day in school. How would he verify the accuracy of his memory so that he can tell whether he has knowledge or is merely romancing? We know that memories err, particularly on details. Would it not be essential, in order to test the accuracy of the memory, to look for some *present* confirmation in records, in objective effects, of what is alleged to have happened, and in other people's *present* reports of their memories? It might be objected that these are merely the means by which the memory of the past event is confirmed. But the point is precisely this, that the means are parts of the continuous and continuing series of effects which make up the history of the event; that they are as genuine parts of its "nature" as anything else; and that an experiment to determine what effects of the past event are yet to be realized in the present or future is necessary before we can acquire genuine knowledge of that aspect of the past.

Before we bring this chapter to a close, something should be said about the wider bearings of Dewey's theory of truth. Its primary purpose is to show that the methods by which truth is won in the sciences are more important than any single result. The understanding of how "truths" come to be accepted inspires us with the confidence that they are better than opinions and with the humility that they are something less than absolute. The genuine issues are not whether ideas work because they are true or are true because they work— two statements which have no pragmatic difference— but whether truths subsist in a world of their own, cut off from time and experience; whether they are private, inaccessible in principle to confirmation by others; whether there are any truths whose validity depends

upon a psychologically immediate grasp of their meaning; whether there are race, class, or religious truths;
whether any method—be it of authority, intuition, or
metaphysics—can yield conclusions equally as reliable
as those of scientific method. To all of these questions
Dewey replies negatively. The denial is not dogmatic
but follows from a positive account of how truths actually make their way in the world of human behavior.
Examine the context in which the scientists accept certain judgments as warranted and reject others as
unwarranted, and the experimental theory of truth, in
its positive claims as well as its negative corollaries,
becomes itself subject to check.

In all of the foregoing, we have been talking about
the prediction of consequences that flow from ideas entertained. But to predict the consequences of an idea or
of a set of ideas is to make an inference. Unless we
make *valid* inferences, the consequences, whether confirmed or not, have no bearing upon the hypothesis or
idea to be tested. They are not genuine consequences.
The question now is: When are inferences valid? By
what principles do we determine the consequences to
expect from a given hypothesis? Are these principles
"true"? The answer to these questions leads us directly
to Dewey's theory of logic.

Chapter

LOGIC AND ACTION

TO those who know him by his less technical writings, John Dewey appears as a great moralist and educator. But his basic doctrines and most fundamental contributions have been in the field of logic. Logic has been his primary intellectual interest for more than forty years. It is safe to predict that his place in the history of science—broadly conceived— will depend upon the influence his conception of logic as the theory of inquiry will exercise upon subsequent generations. Dewey was led to his logical investigations as a result of his attempt to provide a scientific foundation for moral judgments. His specific logical theory, however, may be evaluated independently of his specific ethical insights.

Of all Dewey's contributions, his logical works are the hardest to understand, even for the professional logician. Not so much because of intrinsic difficulties as because they run counter to accepted views from the time of Aristotle to the present. Few are aware of the extent to which common speech is shot through with the classical conceptions of logic—precisely those conceptions which Dewey's theory challenges. When his theory is therefore tested, not in the context of logical operations when we think or behave logically, but in the context of some traditional modes of speech, bewilderment is likely to result. One of the most typical expressions of bewilderment is the statement that Dewey's logical analysis is concerned with everything but logic.

There is a clue to Dewey's logical theory which seems to me to illumine his entire doctrine. It facilitates the understanding of his objective, procedure, and results. The clue is found in an observation or grounded assumption which in practice all of us make—philosophers and nonphilosophers alike. It is the commonplace recognition that *logical* thinking makes a difference. At the very least it makes a difference to what we do and therefore to the state of affairs of which our doing is a part. We are enjoined to think logically wherever thinking is in order. Copybooks and advanced treatises take the maxim with equal seriousness. All enterprise, whether it be in a machine shop, a chess game, or on a field of battle, demands it. That logical thinking counts is one of those first-order truths that we act upon long before we ever formulate it. No one would dream of gainsaying it save in a spirit of paradox. It is one of the chief justifications offered for education. Even statesmen, who would not survive were the habit of logical thinking widespread, must think logically about some things in order to prevent others from doing so.

Strange as it may seem, there has hardly been any theory of logic propounded which does justice to this simple and universally acknowledged fact that logical thinking makes a difference in the world. Indeed, many logical theories have consequences which call this fact into question or make it a mystery that situations could in any way be objectively different as a result of our thinking logically or illogically. And no logical theory

—except Dewey's—has ever offered a remotely plausible account of the very fact so often cited as a reason for the cultivation of logical thought. If we can keep firmly in mind that Dewey is interested in developing a theory that will adequately account for the role which logical thought (action) plays in the world, we will have both a guide to his special doctrines as well as a measure of his achievement.

Logic is often defined with an eye on the special subject matter considered in textbooks as the study of what follows from what, or, more accurately, as the study of the conclusions that may be legitimately inferred from given premises. To the question, what legitimates the inference? the answer is "rules." What legitimates the rules? It is at this point that foundational problems of logic begin. We will briefly consider some of the traditional answers given before presenting Dewey's view.

a) One answer is that logical rules or principles are the formal expression of the ontological or metaphysical structure of "being," where "being" includes everything that is actual and possible. Logical principles state universal and necessary truths about things which are essentially different from the truths established by science. For the latter can only give us probable knowledge. The validity of logical inference is on this view made dependent upon a metaphysical premise which, far from being self-justifying, is itself highly questionable. It is hard to give a specific meaning to "the structure of all possible being." How do we know that there is only one structure? Who has ever canvassed all possible being? Only a finite number of possibilities are ever apprehended. How can we be so certain of all possibilities? Usually, the phrase "all possible being" already defines what is to be admitted as a possibility, so that the position turns out to be purely tautological.

b) Another answer is that logical principles are known by the immediate intuition of the mind. These intuitions are infallible because they have a compulsion which is every whit as strong as the compulsions of our senses. Without them no chain of reasoning can support an argument. A variant view of the same generic type of theory asserts that logical principles are the result of the mind's reflection upon the way in which it necessarily works in ordering its experiences. Logical principles are the forms of our understanding. They express the structure of mind and the structure of things as *known*, but not the structure of existence or being. Fatal difficulties attend this conception of logic. These logical intuitions can no more be guaranteed than any other intuitions, no matter how immediate. Despite the compulsion which they exercise upon human minds, it does not prevent people from entertaining beliefs that are in flat contradiction with each other. As for those who believe that logical principles are forms of the mind, their difficulty is compounded by a mystery. The mystery arises when we try to identify the kind of mind whose forms of activity constitute logical principles. It is not the kind of mind recognized in psychology, sociology, or any other study save that of theology. But no matter what kind of a mind it is, if logical principles are forms of its activity, how do we know that the mind will not change, and with it the allegedly universal and necessary canons of logic?

c) A third view is more poetic and, if taken literally, magical. According to it, the rules of logic are constructions of a developing Self or Mind in which all human beings participate. These rules regulate the creative activity of a great Self. Since whatever exists is the result of such creation, all existence is logical. The order and connection of things is the same as the order and connection of the phases of the Self. In Fichte the Self constructs rules to realize ethical demands, in Schelling to complete aesthetic whole, in Hegel to embrace everything known or even imagined into a supersystem in which every truth entails every other. It is sufficient to observe of this view that it discountenances all the methods by which science acquires piecemeal knowledge of the world without providing us with any more reliable methods of acquiring new knowledge. The Self or Mind of which it speaks is a supernatural entity. Judging by the work it must do, it has usurped the role of God.

d) A fourth view asserts that rules of logic are generalizations from experience. They are no more binding in principle than any other generalization of physics, e.g., that an iron rod will expand when heated. The more often they are confirmed, the more probable they become without ever becoming certain. Logical relations are a mere transcription of what is inherent in nature and, like everything natural, mutable. This is the conception which led John Stuart Mill to say that two plus two equals five might some day be discovered to be true. The great difficulty in this view is to account for propositions which at the outset of its investigation it recognizes as distinctively logical. These propositions are of a form such that their contradictories make no sense in the language in which they are expressed. But all other propositions of physics can be significantly denied, i.e., the denial gives us statements that may be true or false.

These are some typical conceptions of the nature of logic and the source of its validity. It will be noted that all of them have the following two traits in common: (a) they regard logic as a discipline which considers relationships that hold independently of man, and antecedently to human inquiry; (b) none of them can make plausible why logical thinking should make a difference of a specific kind to objective situations in which it is employed.

Dewey's view is that logical forms do not exist in *rerum natura*, nor in consciousness, nor in Self, nor in a Platonic heaven. They arise in the course of *inquiry* and are used as instruments to further inquiry. Any given subject matter acquires logical properties when it is subjected to controlled inquiry. That things and situations can acquire new properties as a result of entering into relationship with other things and activities, is familiar enough. But that these new properties should be logical is a hypothesis never before advanced in developed form in the history of thought. The view that most closely approximates that of Dewey's is the doctrine that the locus of logical relations is *discourse*, that logical propositions are forms of discourse, and that the principles of logic are rules which guide us in deriving one set of statements from another. For Dewey, however, significant discoursing is a way of acting or behaving. When discourse is itself interpreted operationally, it becomes inquiry—an inquiry that involves a manipulation of symbols and ultimately of things. That is why logical discourse makes a difference to behavior and the segment of the world affected by behavior.

But, if logical forms accrue to a subject matter as a result of inquiry, how can they have the binding character, the compulsion and necessity which Dewey, together with all who recognize the autonomy of logic, grants they possess? The answer may be more readily grasped if we consider an analogy from another field. The relations and transactions of human beings with each other is the subject matter of law. Legal principles, however, do not describe nor summarize how human beings in fact do behave. They are rules which regulate, control, permit, or disallow certain aspects of behavior. Behavior becomes legal or illegal wherever it is subject to the activities that define lawmaking and enforcing just as situations become logical or illogical wherever they are controlled by the activities that define inquiry. Logical norms are no more drawn from the blue than are legal norms decrees of God. They represent certain demands upon existing inquiries to which they must conform if they are to achieve the highly warranted results that have been won in some previous inquiry in which these norms were exhibited.

What is inquiry? It is the controlled transformation by the use of symbols (propositions, terms, and relations) of a problematic situation into one in which the relevant elements are so ordered with respect to each other that the initial difficulty is resolved. This definition of inquiry, as well as its general pattern, holds both for common sense and scientific inquiries. These are distinguished from each other in virtue of the distinctive kinds of problems generated by different subject matters and objectives not by any logical difference in the pattern of inquiry or canons of validity. Common-sense inquiry aims directly at the establishment of "objects of use and enjoyment." Scientific inquiry is interested in the establishment of sets of abstract relations, systematically related in respect to each other. Although not directly instrumental to the achievement of any *specific* object of use and enjoyment, it is potentially capable of bringing into existence entire classes of such objects.

What is the pattern of inquiry which enables us to mark it off from mere groping, guessing, or shooting in the dark?

(i) Every inquiry begins within a specific situation which is objectively indeterminate, distinguishable from other situations by some pervasive quality which confers individuality upon it and focuses our interest in one direction rather than another.

(ii) The inquiry proceeds to the discovery of what constitutes the problem—the location of the trouble. This is not always an easy task. Progress toward recognizing the problem is made by noting whether or not distinctions and relationships discovered to have held in previous inquiries of similar situations which have terminated successfully, are present in this situation.

(iii) Relevant ideas are entertained as possible ways of solving the problem. These ideas, embodied in symbols, "are anticipated consequences (forecasts) of what will happen when certain operations are executed under and with respect to observed conditions." This does not mean that first "the facts in the case" are established, and then a suggestion crops up which matures into a hypothesis that will explain them. For ideas and hypotheses direct observation. The facts in the case are just as often established as a result of the hypotheses entertained as are hypotheses suggested by the observed facts. "Observation of facts and suggested meanings or ideas arise and develop with each other." They check and countercheck on each other in order to determine what the problem is, what the facts really are, what would constitute in this specific situation a relevant solution.

(iv) The meaning of the entertained hypothesis, formulated in a proposition, is by a symbolic operation translated into a set of equivalent propositions. This is what Dewey calls "reasoning." It tracks down the inter-relationships between ideas until an idea is reached which has a more direct bearing upon the problem than the original idea, in that acting upon it we get evidence one way or the other for the possible solution. Through reasoning, "an hypothesis, once suggested and entertained, is developed in relation to other conceptual structures until it receives a form in which it can instigate and direct an experiment that will disclose precisely those conditions which have the maximum possible force in determining whether the hypothesis should be accepted or rejected."

(v) The performance of the experiment is the next phase of inquiry. It is an experiment and not a series of blind motions because the preliminary work of ordering data and meanings in respect to each other has already been done. To say that something is an experiment means, then, that we have achieved some knowledge of relevant features of the problem under investigation and that we can indicate in advance what future observations to expect if our hypothesis is valid. An experiment always involves a modification or reordering, of a literally physical kind, of the elements of the problematic situation. The specific modifications, of course, will depend upon the situation. We may put a substance into a flame in order to discover its spectrum line. We cannot put a star into a flame but we can set up our instruments and make the required readings. Setting up the instruments and even putting our bodies, which are also instruments of observation, into a certain position, is a physical action which objectively alters the conditions from which we started.

(vi) The inquiry comes to a close when the difficulties out of which the problem has arisen are settled. What constitutes the settlement of a problem, i.e., the exact degree of confirmation which a hypothesis must receive to be validated, varies from field to field. But in every case the original situation is transformed into one which is more unified, in which discontinuities, stops, and blockages to action have been removed or eased.

This theory of inquiry explains how and why logical thinking makes a difference to things. For the transition from doubt to warranted belief "is achieved by means of operations of two kinds which are in functional correspondence with each other." The first is made up of operations involved in observation of what exists in this particular case under inquiry; the second is the possible and, when acted upon, the actual, operations upon things which define the meaning of any proposed solution to the problem. As a result of these operations, what is inquired into changes in time.

What puzzles many is not the truth of this account of inquiry but its relevance to logical theory. Logic, they say, is the theory of proof, not the theory of inquiry. The latter must be controlled by the former before it can claim validity. At best, Dewey has described the pattern of scientific inquiry and thrown light upon some of the methods by which new knowledge is won. But this already presupposes the possession of norms of valid implication and inference which cannot be derived from existing inquiries, past, present, or future.

This states rather neatly a challenge which Dewey is prepared to meet by arguing that the theory of proof is part of the theory of inquiry, that forms of implication and inference acquire validity by functioning as "leading principles" of inquiry, and that the separation of the theory of logic as proof from scientific inquiry (sometimes called applied logic) not only is inadequate but leads to obvious inconsistencies.

To prove a proposition is literally to test it, and a proved proposition is a tested one. The testing of statements is just as much a part of the process of inquiry as the testing of a thermometer is part of the process of its manufacture. In all testing, certain standards are directly employed. The end product must meet the conditions set by the standard before it is approved. But the standards themselves, from whence are they derived and what is the source of their authority? Dewey's answer is that they are selectively derived from the continuum of inquiries; and that they function regulatively whenever they are explicitly set up as a guide to subsequent inquiry. Why are certain standards set up rather than others to regulate and to test ongoing inquiries? The answer leads us to the doctrine of "leading principles," originally found in Peirce and developed by Dewey.

Human beings make inferences as naturally, even if not so frequently, as they eat, drink, and make merry. These inferences fall into various classes which may be distinguished from each other by the kind of habit of reasoning which each class of inferences illustrates. Usually we are not aware of the habit which leads us to infer certain conclusions from certain premises, given or taken. When we make this habit explicit by stating it in verbal form, it becomes a rule of inference or a leading principle of the class of inferences in question. We observe that these classes of inference differ among themselves. Where premises from which we start are true, different habits of inference lead us to conclusions which are always true, or mostly true, or mostly false, or always false. When these habits operate in inquiries, we notice that they give varying kinds of results. The first two classes of inference "yield conclusions that are stable and productive in further inquiries"; the second two do not. Reflection upon this leads us to establish in explicit linguistic form the leading principles of the first two classes of inference as canons or rules of valid inference by which all types of inference are controlled and judged. They function as "conditions to be satisfied such that knowledge of them provides a principle of direction and of testing." Once established, they have a normative and necessary character. They are binding in a way which is analogous to the binding character of a legal rule finally established to adjudicate a certain class of cases. They are binding, even if certain inferences which are illogical lead to a true conclusion, just as legal rules are binding, even though certain acts which are illegal lead to a just conclusion, i.e., adjudication satisfactory to all parties concerned.

Logical results, then, owe their necessity to the fact that we establish them as methodologically *a priori*. But *we* establish them because of the evidence that these rules and the habits of inference of which they are the explicit formulation enable us to solve more problems than any others. They are necessary but are not absolute because other rules may be formulated for other habits of inference, and there is no guarantee that the methodological *a priori* which *we* have established as a condition that valid inferences must meet, will continue to give us sound and fruitful inquiries. We may speak of rules of inference as "true," but they are not true in the way any premise or conclusion of an argument is "true"; they are true in the way in which a certain method of purifying steel is better adapted than another method to give us material out of which to make a flexible blade. We may call these rules "conventional" if we are prepared to call "conventional" the existence of inquiry, and indeed of every phase of human culture which sets up certain standards that activities must live up to before they are regarded as valid.

No metaphysical assumption about the nature of "reality" is required to account for the "necessity" of logical leading principles. Different deductive systems based upon different rules of inference, each carrying within it its own type of necessity may be elaborated even before a specific occasion in inquiry arises in which they can function, just as an instrument maker may devise tools for use in possible situations even before the need for their use becomes urgent. The study and preparation of various types of possible systems of logical relationships is the special task of symbolic logic and logical syntax.

The chief alternative to Dewey's naturalistic theory of logical principles, or to a similar theory, is to hold that some rules of inference and implication are self-evidently valid, basic to all inquiry because independent of any inquiry, and constituting a realm of pure timeless forms in no way affected by the nature of things or human activities. The alternative is literally a supernatural theory. Yet it cannot escape admitting that logical principles or forms are *applied* to existential material and that they are integral to the procedures of scientific method which result in grounded conclusions about temporal things. If logic is in its first intention pure, i.e., valid independently of all or any subject matter, how can it ever be applied? How can those who hold the supernatural theory of logic consistently speak of "applied logic" without admitting that the subject matter to which logic is applied acquires logical form? Subject matter acquires logical form; it does not have it prior to inquiry, but only as a result of the way in which it is organized by operations that define inquiry. To contrast "logic *and* scientific method" is illegitimate and confusing. "For scientific method both constitutes and discloses the nature of logical forms."

In fact Dewey's logical theory is the most ambitious attempt ever made to formulate the rationale of modern scientific method. Traditional logical theory is very largely derived from the Aristotelian philosophy of science which, although adequate enough to the Greek conception of knowledge and nature, is fundamentally incompatible with the assumptions and procedures of modern science. The Greek theory of nature lost its hold upon the Western world with the rise of experimental science, but the classical theory of logic, which was an integral part of the theory of nature, was retained with minor modification. The attempt to force the logical forms of modern inquiry into the explanatory categories of classical thought is the chief source, according to Dewey, of theoretical confusion in many contemporary accounts of the logic of science.

What are the central differences between the Greek and modern conceptions of nature which should reflect themselves in the Greek and modern conceptions of knowledge and inquiry? Only the briefest indication can be given here. First of all, on the Aristotelian theory natural species or kinds were regarded as definable by "essential qualities" that were inherent and necessary. Only these qualities could be *truly* known by an immediate rational insight. All quantitative variations were considered "accidents," having no necessary connection with the metaphysically real essences which constituted the substance of things and which were accessible only to the inferior knowledge of the senses. In modern science, quantitative determination and variation are central. Things have no essential qualities. Whatever qualities are taken to define scientific objects are "correlations of functional correspondence of changes." Measurements and measuring, therefore, which, according to the Greeks, fell outside the rational order of things, play a tremendous role in modern scientific inquiry. Measurement as a directed form of physical behavior becomes part of the process by which we acquire knowledge of things. Secondly, Greek science was not only qualitative but teleological, i.e., it held that "*knowable* change tends toward a limiting fixed end." The fixed end was its *proper* end. The order of nature was therefore not only rational but moral. In modern science the ends of development are but closes or completions of one series and beginnings of another. Thirdly, in the Aristotelian theory of science every genuine scientific object was self-contained, essentially independent of external or environing things, realizing its form in a virtue of a self-acting, recurrent, qualitative force. Relations are as accidental as quantity. In modern science, all propositions are relational. So are the meanings of the terms related in propositions. "Taking both measurement and relations into account, it is not too much to say that what Greek science and logic rejected are now the head cornerstone of science."

An acceptable theory of logic cannot content itself with minor reforms of the classical tradition, which was grounded in the science of antiquity. It must base itself upon the outstanding features of modern experimental science whose methods have given us our most warranted conclusions. More specifically, it must recognize, according to Dewey, the role of material instruments, techniques, and operations (improvements within which have carried even theoretical science to new levels) as constitutive parts of the pattern of inquiry. It must recognize that both the data and problems of modern science have been a function of the use of instruments in scientific inquiry. It must recognize that the development of modern mathematics and other conceptual tools of analysis was partly the result of the challenge presented by new scientific data and problems, and that, in the light of the history of scientific inquiry, it becomes the sheerest dogmatism to set up some basic scheme of mathematical or logical relations to which the world, or, more accurately, the intellectual behavior of the scientist, *must* conform. A genuinely empirical theory of logic must be a theory of the action scientists engage in, an action on things and on symbols, in acquiring reliable and *grounded* knowledge of the world in which we live.

All effective thinking is thinking to a purpose. It seeks to resolve the difficulties in a specific situation by the use of propositions which direct the course of inquiry. These propositions Dewey considers as *means* to an end—the accomplishment that marks the close of the problem. The means do not always lie at hand; they must be sought for. And when they do lie at hand, as a result of having been placed there in previous inquiry, they must be tested or examined for their relevance and efficacy in a particular inquiry. It is this emphasis upon the means-end or -consequence relation in inquiry which leads Dewey to stress the functional interrelatedness as well as distinctiveness of observational activity and conceptual elaboration.

We can think logically or rationally about anything. Always, when we do so, we are able to discern that some connection has been discovered or established between means and the intended effects (or ends) which have been realized as a consequence of their use. "Rationality as an abstract conception is precisely the generalized idea of the means-consequence relation as such." Means may be used without relation to the end in view; and an end may be "thought about" without concern about the means necessary to its achievement. In the latter case, we have daydreaming; in the former, magic. "The principle of magic is found whenever it is hoped to get results without intelligent control of means." Intelligent control of means demands the organization of materials and the institution of observations in the light of some anticipated way of acting on them; the anticipations of acting one way or another are controlled both by their internal consistency *and* their ability ultimately to put the materials in shape in such a way that the original difficulty is eliminated. The propositions which describe what the facts in the case are at any time and enable us to locate the problem are *material means;* the propositions which direct us to certain operations on the material of observation, leading to consequences which constitute a resolved situation, are called *procedural means.* Both material means and procedural means are *means* because they are formulated with respect to settling a problem, and because they are formulated with respect to each other. Undirected activity and observation, accompanied by the expectation of getting the "proper" results, are only one form of belief in magic; to expect to solve problems about the world by reasoning alone, without some kind of activity subject to the control of observation, is just as much a commitment to the principle of magic.

Chapter

VI

BODY, MIND, AND BEHAVIOR

ONE of the primary difficulties in understanding Dewey's conception of logic as the theory of inquiry, is the tendency to interpret inquiry as if it were a mental process unfolding *in* the mind. On such an interpretation the changes involved in logical inquiry occur inside an individual's head, which is presumably the locus of mind. They may be relevant to the historical career of whatever is inside that head but cannot have a bearing upon the historical career of anything outside of it. Unless, of course, the head swells to include everything, which state of expansive swell-headedness is philosophically known as "subjectivism."

That such an interpretation is caricature follows not merely from Dewey's express disavowal of it but from the fact that it runs absolutely counter to his description of mind as denoting a set of differential activities of the body, habituated socially and historically, in, by, and through an environment. His naturalistic approach to mind is present or assumed in almost everything he has written from the time he abandoned Hegelianism about fifty years ago. In outline it is the most far-reaching and yet most sophisticated type of behaviorism that has been developed. "Sophisticated" in the sense that it neither denies nor burks any observably experienced quality of human conduct, although it does challenge some conventional modes of speech about "consciousness" when these are literally construed, as they often are. In passing, it should be noted that two of the most important movements in modern psychology, the functionalism of Angell and the early behaviorism of Watson, drew a considerable part of their inspiration from Dewey's psychological writings. I do not think it is an exaggeration to state that Dewey's stature as a philosopher has overshadowed his stature as a psychologist.

It is not only Dewey's theory of logic which requires an empirical theory of mind. As we shall see in the sequel, his educational, moral, and aesthetic doctrines are securely rooted in the view that whatever psychic processes are (and he does not deny their existence), they are distinguishable only by their differential observable effects on something which in the first instance is not psychical at all, and from which they emerge as qualities dependent upon the way in which the non-psychical is organized. Changes in the life of man as a thinking creature no longer appear mysterious, and an approach is indicated by which the human mind and society can be not only understood but intelligently controlled.

Consider, for example, some of the consequences that have been drawn in the history of thought from the dualistic assumption, against which the main incidence of Dewey's psychological analysis has been directed, that mind is a substance or power, separate from the body and its environment. At once the momentous issues involved in the question of mind-body come into the light. The dualistic theory has prepared the way for the belief that certain indisputable truths about the human mind are disclosed to direct inspection, and that

they are not subject to the controls and empirical tests
of methods of inquiry so fruitful in other fields. Among
the truths so disclosed, it has often been argued, are
"moral truths" of the greatest importance to human
welfare—personal and social. By locating "the essential personality" in a mind or consciousness, discon-
tinuous with the world of matter or nature, the
consoling doctrine has been fostered that human beings
in their "innermost selves" can never be compelled except by forces to which they voluntarily submit and
which are therefore not really compelling; that human
beings are "frèe" not in virtue of a power to do or to
refrain from doing, but in virtue of mere assent or intention. Behind the argument that a man is always free
to work or not to work under a given wage scale, always
free to criticize those who enjoy a monopoly of power in
a given region or country, always free to live or die—
has been the tacit commitment to a dualistic view of
mind-body. From it flows the stern but intellectually
easy moralism that no man (or woman) can escape
responsibility for anything he does when he is faced by
hunger or terror, and that we, who observe him, can
never be absolved from the responsibility of passing
judgment on him.

Even more fateful is the use to which this dualistic
theory of mind-body has been put in urging that significant social change can only come from change within
the individual soul or self. Down to our own day, eloquent spokesmen for powerful cultural and religious
groups have counterposed "the revolution within" to
fundamental institutional reforms. Men, we have been
told, must make themselves over by purer thought, or
by more kindly feeling or by a moral rededication as a

necessary precedent to any social change which will
not bring back old evils in new form. Indeed, there are
no evils, as distinct from accidents or human limitations, except those which individuals have been guilty
of committing. We must therefore look to saintliness
not science for our cures.

Not all who hold the dualistic view are aware of it.
But wherever knowledge is divorced from action or
theory from practice, wherever action and practice are
regarded as something which compromises the purity,
the objectivity, the perfection of knowledge and theory,
wherever the exigencies of living in a material world
are deplored as a trial imposed on "the spirit," wherever faith is separated from works and ends from
means, the dualistic theory of mind-body will be found
lurking among the unexamined assumptions.

In challenging the dualistic theory, Dewey has challenged one of the most pervasive determinants of Western European culture, an attitude fortified by religion,
by popular morality, by the teachings of the Academy
as well as of the Learned Doctors. It is not surprising,
therefore, that it is Dewey's theory of human nature
and human mind which has provoked the charge of materialism against him, particularly in theological quarters. If refusal to dissociate mind from body and body
from nature is materialism, Dewey is one of the greatest materialists of all time. Nor would Dewey hesitate
to call himself a materialist, were materialism not such
an ambiguous doctrine in formulation if not in intent.
There are materialisms which deny the existence of
mind on the ground that only matter is "real"; there
are materialisms which deny that thinking has any observable effects, on the ground that only matter can

causally influence matter. For Dewey, such statements
cannot be given any empirical meaning, i.e., meanings
which can be confirmed or falsified by scientific evidence. But he does share with materialism its intent
and cultural motivation. These are derived from a basic
desire to investigate the "mysteries of the soul" by
methods of scientific inquiry which in principle cannot
recognize any dualistic separation of mind and body,
in order that human behavior and society may be more
intelligent, more humane, and free. Dewey tries to ac-
complish what materialism set out to do without com-
promising the attempt at the very beginning by calling
into question the existence of the psychic qualities
under investigation.

It is the very prevalence, however, of certain modes
of speech (whose origin we need not here investigate)
about the self, mind, and consciousness in the everyday
language of even professional behaviorists which makes
Dewey's approach to mind difficult to grasp. We speak
of "*the* self" as if it were a self-contained entity distinct, and sometimes separate, from our body and its
ways of action. We say that thoughts are "in the
mind" or that an individual has "lost" his consciousness or mind as if they were immaterial substances, and
so on. Taken literally, and they often are, such expressions testify to the strength of the dualistic view
that whatever exists falls into two mutually exclusive
and unbridgeable segments, variously called the world
of matter and the world of mind, nature and experience, the physical and the psychical, scientific objects
and sense data, environment and .consciousness. To be
sure, there are certain classes of empirical facts which
can be interpreted to lend support to this sharp dual-

ism between the world of nature and the world of mind. But it is obvious that these empirical facts do not compel such an interpretation. More important, the interpretation is such that it is incompatible with myriads of events in which mind and body appear, not as substances of different kinds, but as adjectival distinctions within a continuous process of natural behavior. It is in virtue of the different qualities and effects revealed in one and the same world of objects and events that we say this acts now like a lump of matter, now like an animal blinded by a glare of light, now like a member of a civilized community.

By his emphasis upon the continuity of nature, body, society, and mind, Dewey does two things. He breaks down the dualism between the physical and the psychical without reading the properties of mind into nature, as do the mentalists and panpsychists, and without denying the existence of consciousness, as do extreme materialists and behaviorists. Secondly, he is able to make clear that "the unity of the human being" consists not in the sum of separate ultimate elements, whether these be sensations or reflexes, ideas or glandular secretions, but in an observable series of co-operative functions, a working together of interacting processes, that constitute a personality.

The dualism between the physical and psychical is overcome by positive analysis of a double sort. Mental behavior is shown to involve in an integral way not only the brain but the body, and not only the body but a physical environment, outside of the body skin, which is an integral part of physiological processes. In this manner, Dewey prepares the ground for an understanding of why it is that inquiry makes a difference to the world, i.e., why and how "thought" can be practical. Secondly, the life of mind, its speech and habits, are shown to be involved in an integral way with an historically conditioned social environment. This prepares the ground for Dewey's ethical and social theory, according to which institutional changes become the most effective instruments of liberating the possibilities of individual growth.

That the mind in some sense is dependent upon the brain is universally known. Not so well known is the fact that in the functioning of mind not only the brain but other organs of the body, not to speak of the respiratory and circulatory systems, are involved. And in turn the physiological processes and acts can take place only insofar as they interact with, or adjust to, events outside the boundary of the body. The organism does not find an environment for itself in the way in which a person finds a house in which to live. To be an organism is already to have some physical environment as a natural condition of existence and action. No sharp separation therefore is possible between the physical, the living, or what Dewey calls the psycho-physical, and the mental. Neither, however, are these three identical. They are distinguished from each other in virtue of specifiable, observable properties that are correlated with observable differences in the "complexity and intimacy of interaction among natural events."

The physical, or Matter, Life, and Mind are abstractions, according to Dewey, not existences. Existences have physical, living, or mental character depending upon the set of properties they reveal as they develop in time. The fact that some properties whose conjunction indicates the presence of mind emerge later in time

than others does not make them "less real" or less efficacious than others, as traditional materialism assumed. The fact that under certain circumstances
physical situations are changed as a result of operations and actions that indicate the presence of the
mental, does not justify belief in *a* mind as a separate
power, force, or vital energy which mysteriously acts
upon things, as traditional spiritualism assumed. The
problems about mind-body which have mystified philosophers can only be settled by seeing the elements which
have been originally separated as functional distinctions within a continuity or history of events. "To see
the organism *in* nature, the nervous system in the
organism, the brain in the nervous system, the cortex in
the brain is the answer to the problems which haunt
philosophy. And when thus seen they will be seen to be
in, not as marbles in a box but as events are in history,
in a moving, growing, never finished process."

One of the most impressive features of Dewey's approach to psychological phenomena has been his insistence upon describing their differential qualities in
terms of observable effects. Long before "physicalism"
was proclaimed as a new doctrine by the logical empiricists, Dewey was applying it in a thoroughgoing
manner to the basic categories of life and mind. Observe
the characteristic way in which he interprets the key
terms of "need," "demand," "satisfaction," "sensation," "feeling," and later, "consciousness," "mind,"
"emotions," and "imagination."

The activities of living things are distinguished from
those of nonliving things by the presence of needs.
What are needs? By need is meant "a condition of ten-

sional distribution of energies such that the body is in
a condition of uneasy or unstable equilibrium."

Living bodies are also characterized by "efforts" or
"demands" to satisfy needs. What are efforts or demands? They are "manifested in movements which
modify environing bodies in ways which reach upon the
body, so that its characteristic pattern of active
equilibrium is restored."

Living bodies are also characterized by "satisfactions." What are satisfactions? By satisfaction "is
meant this recovery of equilibrium pattern, consequent
upon the changes of environment due to interactions
with the active demands of the organism."

All of these terms have here a biological significance,
but wherever they are employed in a specifically human
context they are still tied down to observable modes of
action and interaction. But the field of action and interaction is widened to include observable features of
the social environment which is constituted by institutions, other human beings, and meanings expressed in
speech or embodied in things.

The belief in the domain of a private experience
which is open only to direct inspection is most stub-
bornly defended at the point where we speak of sensations, consciousness, mind.

A "sensation," according to Dewey, is not a simple
quality of a psychic event but "a perception of a dis-
criminated quality" in a situation undergoing physical
change of some sort. The perception is not an intuitive
grasp of the quality as a mental event but a discriminating activity of the body as a whole toward something
objectively present as a sign of something else to come.
Red is not a sensation but a quality of a natural event

perceived through the instrument of a sense organ, the eye. A loud tone is not a sensation but a quality of another natural event perceived by the ear. *What* is perceived depends causally upon the objective properties of the sense organs in the same way as the quality of a wound may depend upon the property of the instrument which has produced it. Qualities are not *in* the body; nor are they *in* things. They are found wherever relations and interactions exist between things and other things, things and bodies, and bodies and other bodies.

"Feelings" are qualities of sentient or living things. They emerge whenever the activities of the body which denote its sensitivity and interested reaction are manifest. The more complicated and extensive the selective interactions between organism and the physical world, the more important do feelings become in behavior as marking off sets of new qualities from old. Before thinking begins, they function as organic indicators, of varying degrees of reliability, that "all's well" or "something's wrong." They are marks of qualitative individuality. "Feeling" is "a name for the coming to existence of those ultimate differences in affairs which mark them off from one another and give them discreteness; differences which upon the physical plane can be spoken of only in anticipation of subsequent realization, or in terms of different numerical formulae, and different space-time positions and contiguities."

"Consciousness" is the most ambiguous of all psychological terms. Sometimes it refers to the presence of feelings where feelings are had but not known. Sometimes it refers to the perception of meanings. In this last sense, human beings *are* conscious; they do not

literally *have* consciousness in the way a man has hair
or a hat. To *be* conscious is to take note of the meanings of things and by means of organic activity to redirect them.

"Mind" is also an activity. It is minding. Its activity
differs from that of consciousness in that it operates as
a set of organized meanings that have been built up as a
result of previous activities. To have a mind is to have
a store of systematized meanings already at hand to
develop or restrain the conscious action which goes off
like a shot at the perception of a meaning.

Dewey's descriptions of the basic categories of life
and mind have been given as illustrations of the way he
persistently links up the psychic processes of man with
the physical world. His procedure is the same in treat-
ing other psychological concepts like imagery, memory,
will, and emotion. Unfortunately his psychological discussions are scattered throughout his various writings,
and nowhere systematically developed. To a large extent they are programmatic, lacking the details which
are so necessary to convert an insight into a directing
hypothesis. In addition, the language in which they are
couched varies from time to time as has the language
of psychology itself in the last fifty years. But there is
one characteristic principle which runs through all of
Dewey's psychological writings, whether he is discussing
the reflex arc, states of consciousness, the stimulus-re-
sponse bond, pulses of neural energy, exteroceptor and
muscular activities. This is the principle that perceptual awareness has no fixed quality when it is considered independently of its functional context in the
process of adaptation to and *readaptation* of a changing environment by an organism. Whatever quality it

has depends upon the things to which it refers, the effects it produces, the function it plays in experience—where experience means a series of acts and transactions between man and the world. From this principle follows Dewey's rejection of psychological atomism, whether it be phrased in introspective or behavioral terms. There is no fundamental or ultimate element out of whose combinations the various mental traits are born. The simple, the pure, the clear, the distinctive characters of mental behavior which lend themselves to psychological system-building are derived as end-products or results of complex activities undertaken by the organism as a whole. As Dewey puts it in one of his formulations: "Immediately, every perceptual awareness may be termed indifferently emotion, sensation, thought, desire: not that it *is* immediately any one of these things, or all of them combined, but that when it is taken in some *reference*, to conditions or to consequences or to both, it has, in that contextual reference, the distinctive properties of emotion, sensation, thought or desire."

So far we have indicated the manner in which psychical characters involve and integrate the physical world. It becomes clear now why thought and inquiry can be practical. Man, a creature of nature, can, by using natural means, within limits, change it. The possibility is always there; the invitation to act on it renewed whenever problems arise. The history of cultures contains the record of how men have acted on it in the past: but the history of philosophy, by playing all the changes on the theme of mind-body dualism, has made a mystery of how that record came to be made.

That thinking has practical effects is a natural fact. The directions of thinking, the ends it serves, the choices determining whether steel should go into school buildings or sixteen-inch guns—these are natural, too. But natural, as distinctively *social* phenomena, not physical. In his human estate man is a psycho-physical-social creature. Only one half the story has been told in tracing the involvements of body, physical world, and psyche; the other half concerns the even more intimate relationship between the psychical and the social. Nor is the whole story the result of mechanically adding the halves together. For man's social life influences those psychical processes which we have hitherto considered only in interaction with the physical world; and it is obvious that physical factors and conditions have a far-reaching influence upon many features of any culture. But the tentative distinction between the psychical-physical and the psychical-social is adopted for purposes of exposition. Psycho-physical behavior is the matrix out of which inquiry as a natural process, effecting changes in other processes, develops; psycho-social behavior is the matrix out of which meanings, moral intent, and personal quality crystallize. For Dewey, both are continuous. As a naturalist, he accepts the findings of science that the physical has temporal priority. But as far as man is concerned, the social is the widest and most complex mode of association into which man as a psycho-physical creature can enter. It is in social life that almost all of the qualities that we regard as distinctively human appear. And, as we shall see, in indicating wherein "the unity of the human being" lies, main emphasis falls upon the quality of interpersonal relationships which are found in the realm of the social.

How do social determinants enter in affecting the character of psychological processes? Here we suffer from an embarrassment of riches as far as illustrative material from Dewey's writings is concerned. We shall briefly indicate his approach to habit, emotion, and thought.

Habits are acquired ways of action whose patterns repeat themselves in time. Their locus *seems* to be always strictly individual. Their causes, meaning, and consequences are not. For habits have histories. These histories are the result not merely of repeated acts of the organism; they are the story of the regulations and controls of action by family, community, state. Habits therefore are social; and to the extent to which we define conduct, character, personality, self, will, or any other meaningful aspect of human behavior in terms of habits, the individual is a social product. He can only be understood in relation to his culture and its institutions. The dualism between individual and society disappears at the first glance. *Conflicts* between individuals and society are another matter. They testify to modes of interaction, not separation. The actual locus of habits, therefore, turns out to be relationships between people. Except to a biologist, *what* a man is, literally depends upon what other people are. And even a biologist must often take note of the social relations between people to account for what he finds in body behavior.

Except for physiological processes and certain reflexes like the knee-jerk or blinking, the native behavior of man is always discovered by an analysis of his acquired behavior. The capacity to fight, the capacity to sing, the capacity to love, and the mechanisms appropriate to them, are natural to man. The fight*ing*, the lov*ing*, the sing*ing* depend upon permissive conditions of the social environment. What, when, and how one fights, sings, or loves depends almost wholly upon the social institutions—"the embodied habits" of past and present—which already exist when the organism comes on the scene.

By pointing to the pervasiveness of habits and their historical character, Dewey is able to cut the ground from under the hoary but still very much alive belief in the unalterability of human nature. The facts of heredity be what they are, changes in social conditions will produce those changes in men which are socially and morally significant. It is in social and moral terms that human nature is always construed, especially by those most convinced of its fixity. We do not have to "abolish the laws of Mendelian heredity," as the popes of Soviet biology have proclaimed, in order to improve the quality of human conduct any more than we have to intervene surgically to teach children the social amenities. War has many modes, ranging from gladiatorial combat to gas and aerial attack by participants who do not even see each other. Is there any single impulse to which all these variations in waging war, so disparate in causes and effects, can be reduced? Some grant that the variations are socially determined but that war, as a form of violent action, (as well as other institutions like property, the family, the state) is rooted in the natural endowment of man. But the natural endowment of man shows at most a capacity for violent action. Whether the capacity expresses itself in shedding blood according to certain rules or in any of William James's moral equivalents of war depends upon the set of habits which obtains in a culture, and upon the historical context of those habits. "War is thus seen to be a function of social institutions, not of what is natively fixed in human constitution."

Few would dispute that habits are social; but few realize what the implications are for social theory and ethics of recognizing them as social. We shall return to them later. But that emotions, as Dewey claims, are also social would be very much disputed. To some, emotions are private and irreducible qualities of "inner experience"; to others, they are observable accompaniments of bodily changes. To Dewey, emotions as well as sensations have their physiological correlates and causes, but he distinguishes emotions from sensations, in that emotional behavior always involves a response directed toward another human being. Sometimes the response is indirect as when things that have been associated with persons in past relationship stir emotion. Grief is not something which is "deeper" introspectively or more complex viscerally than pain. Its context is wider than the physical and psycho-physical interactions which give the experience of pain, for it extends beyond the boundary of the body and physical space to include personal social relations. It is what human beings do or leave undone which evokes emotions. The scientific treatment of the emotions is incomplete unless the maladjustments, conflicts, and integrations of face-to-face, interpersonal relationships are investigated with the same care as intrabodily changes.

That thinking is as much a form of social behavior as it is of psycho-physical behavior was already made clear in our discussion of Dewey's theory of ideas. Thinking involves speech and "speech is just what men *do* when they communicate with others or with themselves." We can communicate by gestures, symbols, or sounds, provided they effectively indicate what we propose to do. The effective indication is tested by the behavioral response of others. The stock of meanings we already have, the methods of testing and communicating them, the processes of forging and fixating new meanings—are all social. As we have already seen, the social basis of thinking, and of every conscious or meaningful phase of behavior, is emphasized to correct the view that thinking is a purely organic response to a stimulus expressed in speech habits ranging from overt to whispered, and from whispered to implicit or silent. The heart of Dewey's view, which had been independently developed by his great disciple and colleague, George Herbert Mead, is that both "habits" and "speech" are social, and that the evidences of social habits are literally present in the most private thoughts of the most isolated spectator.

From another side, Dewey reaches the same conclusion by way of an analysis of the nature of "the stimulus." The conventional scientific statement that behavior is a response to a given stimulus does not suggest the initiating role of the organism in determining what the stimulus is. If response waits on stimulus, we have a conception of human life as something completely determined by events outside of the body. It is true that an organism is always given with and in an environment. The environment as a whole, however, is never a stimulus. The selective activity of the body, directed to some point of change in the environment, determines what the stimulus is. We recognize the stimulus only after an initial response has been made. At any given moment, thousands of things are potential stimuli to a human creature with a certain history. At any given time, what it is doing is part of a series of acts, some already completed and others in process. Behavior is a serial process, response is a change in behavior, and the stimulus a specific environmental (or organic) change which is related in some way to the already existing preoccupation and interested activity of the organism. It is not the state of the organism as a whole but the *activity* of the organism as a whole to which the stimulus is related. Any event that produces a change in the activity of the organism as a whole, anything which must be attended to because its influence involves something already going on, is a stimulus. The direction in which it reorients the pattern of behavior is due as much to the nature of the pattern as to its own qualities.

In what way does this analysis of the "stimulus" affect the concept that thought is purely an organic reaction? In this: ideas, as plans of action, which express meanings that are socially derived, determine what aspects of the environment are stimuli (or data). The recognition that something is a stimulus means that we have already begun to think or act. And since the ideas, the plans of action, are drawn from our social world, what we discover to be stimuli, whenever thought is in question, depends largely upon the society in which we live, its attitudes, values, and "embodied habits." A bushman and an Eskimo, an Englishman and a Zulu, an American and a Japanese, would not always receive the same stimuli, even if they found themselves in the same environment.

All of us are vaguely aware that a normal human being functions as a unity. That is to say, there is an integral quality of behavior which is not found when we describe the functioning of the separate parts of the body—skin, muscles, nervous system, glands; nor when we add to this accounts of emotions, will, habit, mind. A human being is a "person" and when we say that an individual is "limited," "overspecialized," "at odds with himself," "neurotic," "dissociated," we mean that he is less of a person than when he is "integrated," "many-sided," "harmoniously developed," "sane." One of the reasons that belief in the "soul" has persisted is that many people have sought to find a definite locus for the bond of unity that marks the presence of personality. Not finding it in any one phase of bodily or psychic activity, they have postulated the existence of a nonobservable entity, and offered as evidence for its existence their vague and unanalyzed feeling that a human being is more than blood *and* nerves, *and* memories *and* habits. Many philosophers who have been too sophisticated to believe in the "soul" because of its role in the religious mythology of Western Europe have substituted in its stead terms that are less theological but no less mysterious. Thus, Kant's "transcendental unity of apperception" is partly designed to restore the unity of the self which had been destroyed by Hume's analysis of the self as a series of impressions. Even some popular philosophers and psychologists in our own day, like Freud, proceed in the same way insofar as they conceive of the "unconscious" as a substance or receptacle in which are stored repressed desires and instinctive drives.

For Dewey, the unity of the organism, considered biologically, consists in the way in which all parts of the body *function together* to produce the balance or moving equilibrium that we call the quality of good health. But since man is not only a biological organism but a social creature, his unity as a *human* being consists in the co-operative functioning of his relationships to other human beings in a social environment. Where these are disturbed, neurotic tangles, "withdrawals from reality," and psychoses result. Sometimes the consequences manifest themselves in a breakdown of the unity of the organism. Sicknesses that appear physical may have their origin in frustrations in human relationships, worries, ungratified needs for social and personal security in times of danger. The integrated or truly unified human being, Dewey concludes, is one whose life is integrated with the social environment, the persons and institutions which are the objects of his rational and voluntary loyalties. It is not the social environment in the abstract or at large in which this co-operative interaction must take place, but the specific society in which the individual works, plays, and loves. A society so organized that it makes practically impossible a rational distribution of the social opportunities for significant work, and of the material and ideal goods that are so necessary to co-operative agreements as well as to fruitful disagreements between human beings, is a society which breeds disintegrated and crippled personalities. Some are crippled by excess of power; others by timidity. Some by deficiency of emotion; others by emotionalism. The unity of the human being, then, is a social problem as much as it is a psychological one. If Dewey's theory of human nature and conduct is sound, the proximate instrumentalities for bringing the conditions into existence which will produce the greatest number of integrated personalities are to be found in social action and movements for social change. He asks in a question which is its own answer: "Is there anything in the whole business of politics, economics, morals, education—indeed in any profession—save the construction of a proper human environment that will serve, by its very existence, to produce sound and whole human beings, who in turn will maintain a sound and healthy human environment?"

Chapter

VII

STANDARDS, ENDS, AND MEANS

JOHN DEWEY'S moral theory is continuous with his theory of inquiry and human behavior. But it is in his moral theory that the revolutionary consequences of his philosophy appear in their most vital impact upon everyday affairs. He does not moralize, or exhort, or paint a picture of the good life for the professionally virtuous. Nor does he offer a recipe book of ethical precepts to be used as a guide in settling human troubles. Instead he sketches a method of approach which enables those who adopt it to get an insight into the way moral judgments function and therewith to test their moral judgments scientifically.

The very phrase "to test moral judgments scientifically" seems to couple two things which the major traditions of philosophy have usually kept apart. Absolutists have taught that the ultimate ends of human conduct are sanctioned either by intuition or revelation or conscience; that their validity does not depend upon methods of scientific inquiry, which at best give probable conclusions only about matters of fact, i.e., about "what is" rather than about "what should be." The theological brethren of the absolutists have been even more forthright about the matter. "What we need," they cry, "are saints not scientists." Relativists have contended that the ultimate ends of human conduct are sanctioned, if at all, by some arbitrary social or personal fiat—power or desire or emotion. As Bertrand Russell has put it in one of his philosophic moods: "Science has nothing to say about 'values'. . . . Questions as to 'values' lie wholly outside the domain of knowledge . . . when we assert that this or that has 'value' we are giving expression to our own emotions."

This stark opposition between experience and the ideals by which experience is evaluated, between the realm of nature and the realm of value, is the answer most frequently made by both the high priests of religion and popular science to the central problem of philosophy. According to Dewey, "the central problem of philosophy is the relation that exists between the beliefs about the nature of things due to natural science to beliefs about values—using that word to designate whatever is taken to have rightful authority in the direction of conduct." It is not only the central problem of philosophy; it is the deepest problem of modern life. "The problem of restoring integration and co-operation between man's beliefs about the world in which he lives and his beliefs about the values and purposes that should direct his conduct is the deepest problem of modern life."

In the field of science, a general pattern of inquiry has been developed which is competent to integrate and test our beliefs about the nature of the world. Can a similar method be worked out for the field of moral evaluations which, without invoking any supernatural element, will make moral decisions more intelligent, better grounded, less subject to caprice? Dewey's hypothesis is that the rationale of scientific method is just as applicable to the field of morals as to the world of nature, and that in any particular situation, by the use of intelligent methods of analysis, one course of conduct can be established as "better" than another.

The conduct which we call morality does not wait for moral theory in order to come into existence, any more than logical activity waits upon a theory of logic to develop. In every society there are approved ways and disapproved ways of doing things. Morals are as universal, and as variable, as custom and habit. And like customs and habits, they are as unconscious. They reach the plane of reflective morality when customs are challenged by other customs, or when the influence of new inventions, new ideas, new difficulties, makes it impossible for the old and familiar customs to provide the easy guidance they have furnished in the past. At this point the problem arises: What ought we to do? The quest for standards, ends, ideals, principles begins. For what we do depends, at least in part, upon the standards or ends we consider valid.

Almost at once, however, the question suggests itself: How are standards or ends themselves to be tested? Granted that moral decisions cannot be made save in the light of some end. Is the mere having or entertaining of a standard or end sufficient? Is a decision morally justified if it is sanctioned by any standard? Any length can serve as the measure of distance. Can any standard serve as the measure of a good life? If it can, its application would in principle be as easy as that of a rule or yardstick. And just as irrelevant to what is distinctively moral in human experience. For deliberation, if it took place at all, would concern itself exclusively with *how* the standard should be applied not *whether* it or some other standard should be applied. Clearly, if standards and ends are above criticism, all of them are on the same level. How could we decide between them? What would it mean to say, as we do, that one is "better" than another? Merely, that it is stronger? Or that we like it?

Examine any particular standard or end which is allegedly self-certifying. It has a history. It has a social and personal context. It has definite consequences. The psychological and sociological causes of its acceptance can be discovered. It is incompatible with certain other standards and ends. Has all this no bearing upon the question as to whether we should adopt this standard rather than another?

There are two generic ways in which standards or ends may be criticized. The first is metaphysical, the second empirical. We may say either that standards are justified by a "higher intuition," by the nature of "the Real," by a rule of "Reason" (where "Reason" means formal consistency not scientific inquiry); or that standards are empirically verified in action. The latter view is Dewey's own, but before developing it a few remarks on the first position are necessary to indicate its inadequacy.

To criticize standards or ends by appealing to "a higher intuition" raises the same kind of questions about intuitions that have been asked about values of a "lower" order. Even the highest intuitions are notoriously at odds with each other. Many confess that they are not blessed by an insight that extends to levels higher than the experience of the natural world. No method is indicated by which intuitions can be confirmed in doubtful cases except by a process (sometimes called authentitication or validation to distinguish it from verification) that turns out on analysis to be a technique of passing off private prejudices as public truths. The psychology, the conception of meaning, the theory of nature behind this moral philosophy all presuppose a metaphysics whose basic truths require a special nonempirical method, sometimes even a special organ of knowledge, to be apprehended. Ironically enough, far from escaping the relativism and subjectivism which it lays at the door of the empirical approach to ethics, this school of thought, by multiplying absolutes, gives a principled basis to never-ending conflicts about values.

To test standards by the criterion of logical consistency contributes to bringing home to us their meaning; but, taken by itself, it is primarily a test of our own resoluteness of belief in them rather than an empirical check on their validity. According to this view, any standard would be valid were we prepared to hold it with sufficient ruthlessness.

Those who derive justification of standards from some ontological "Reality" have never succeeded in doing anything else than deducing ends of human conduct from premises into which they have already been unconsciously introduced. Usually the key term "Real" is a disguised value term. Some end or value is assumed to be intrinsically valuable at the very outset, and a metaphysical system is then constructed "to prove" it. It is not hard to show that behind some of the most imposing metaphysical systems in the history of thought has been a desire to preserve some fixed centers of preference and privilege in the process of experience, upon which to hang traditional values of use and enjoyment, so as to remove them forever from the challenge of new, emerging interests. Not infrequently in systems which identify the real, the rational, and the ideal, a "might makes right" doctrine appears as a corollary. The Hegelian dictum that *Die Weltgeschichte is das Weltgericht* is a case in point.

Does Dewey's empirical approach to ethics fare any better? How can ends or standards be tested in action except by applying other ends or standards taken to be final? Dewey's answer to this question is crucial, for it is also an answer to the chief objections that critics have raised. He begins by pointing out that the ends which are here assumed to be final are ideas whose meanings are determined in the same way as other ideas, viz., by their consequences. We cannot say that we really *know* what our ends are before we have reflected upon the probable consequences of carrying them out, as plans of action, in practice. We criticize our ends by inquiring into what results from the use of the *means* designed to realize them. Whenever action is intelligent and responsible, the means are part of the end. We literally do not know the end we have chosen unless we understand the train of relevant consequences involved in bringing that choice about.

But still, one asks, aren't there certain standards or values which we must use in order to determine whether the consequences of acting on our ends, of finding specific means, are satisfactory? Certainly there are. A whole host of them like friendship, wisdom, beauty, courage, health, security, adventure. Yet note: although these goods are assumed to be immediately valid, none of them is taken as finally good. None is supreme, none above the necessity of pointing to consequent goods in case its own presumptive validity is threatened. For it is obvious that the goods of this world are not always in harmony with each other. One good conflicts with another good; knowledge with happiness, serenity with intensity. In no two situations can we resolve the conflict of values in exactly the same way. Hence, although we use the values and standards that have emerged out of previous deliberations as guiding principles of action, of themselves they never can determine the unique good of *this* particular situation. True, without them we should no more know how to find out what we should do than we could begin a scientific inquiry into any matter of fact without some knowledge assumed to be valid. But there is something more always present, or the possibility of something more, which controls the relevance, the manner, and the degree of their application. The good of any situation in which the problem arises as to what *should* be done is something discovered as a result of reflective inquiry, and the objective changes produced by that inquiry. There is no Good in the large any more than there is Truth in the large. That idea is true in any particular situation which is the outcome of the use of scientific methods of inquiry; that proposal is good in any particular situation where evaluations are being evaluated which is the conclusion of controlled inquiry into the available alternatives of action. There are always truths on hand from previous inquiries to aid in testing other candidates for truth. There are always goods and values at hand which are available in testing proposals that are candidates for intelligent choice. But neither the truths, nor the values, which we so employ, are exempt from showing their own credentials if something about the way they function puts it into our heads to ask for them.

Observe now how the other principles of Dewey's philosophy begin to converge on the ethical question. The good of a particular situation is found in that particular reconstruction of affairs which removes the initial difficulty. The initial difficulty involves a conflict of need or interest in an objective situation. Need and interest are not unobservable states of mind but are qualities of behavior, biological and social. Standards and ideals function like scientific hypotheses. They are plans of action. Whether or not they enable us, by controlling the relevant features of the case, to instate the good, is subject to verification. Given a situation of conflict, born out of needs, desires, and lacks; given also a set of ends or standards that offer directions to courses of conduct designed to fulfill these needs, desires, and lacks; then the adequacy of any of the given ends or of new ones to the situation in hand can *in principle* be settled with scientific objectivity.

To speak of the scientific approach to ethics suggests to many that ethics is part of the natural sciences. But since it is obvious that the natural sciences do not concern themselves with statements about what *should* or *ought* to be done, or with judgments as to what is of most worth, such a procedure would be self-defeating. And so it would be were this Dewey's meaning. Dewey, however, maintains not that the subject matter of the physical sciences and the subject matter of ethical science are the same but only that the logic of inquiry into the matter-of-fact propositions of the natural sciences and into the value-propositions of ethical science is of the same generic kind. How, then, does the subject matter of ethics differ from the subject matter of the natural sciences? Dewey's answer is that evaluations of acts of value constitute the subject matter of ethical inquiry. Not the *description* of acts of value, for this is the work of historian and sociologist, but *evaluations* of acts of value. What does it mean to evaluate acts of value? It means to undertake an inquiry which will enable us to say that this act of value, in the light of relevant consequences, is better or worse in relation to the needs and interests of the situation which calls it forth.

The belief that human experience is the source of values and of the methods and standards that test values, aligns Dewey with the tradition of ethical naturalism. But there are currents within this tradition from which Dewey is widely separated. All naturalists stress the importance of interest, desire, and vital impulse in the consideration of value. That values develop out of vital impulses, desires, and interests, Dewey readily admits. That values are constituted by them he denies. Vital impulses by themselves are blind. Without thought we do not know what the object of an impulse really is and whether our action has attained it. Impulses are immediate. Valuations are not. Questions of value arise when impulses conflict. Whether the gratification of this impulse is better than another cannot be decided by impulse but by deliberation. What is valuable is that which is chosen *after* deliberation. "It takes *thought* to convert an impulse into a desire, centered on an object."

Nor is the existence of desire sufficient by itself to justify us in regarding its objects as valuable. "What *ought* I to desire in this particular case?" is the relevant ethical question. In answering this question, we cannot assume that mere desiring instates a value. And empirically, we never do. We discriminate between desires, investigate their contexts and consequences, evaluate them in respect to each other. Unless we ask *what* it is that we desire, the desire is a natural event of whose cause, direction, and object we are ignorant. When we know *what* it is that we desire, it is always possible to link it up with the objective lacks and needs of a specific situation. We can begin to criticize it. As a result of the process of criticism, value is bestowed upon it.

The point becomes focal when we consider a theory which seems at first sight to be close to Dewey's, viz., "A value is any object of any interest." It is good as far as it goes because it suggests some relation between objects and interests. But it does not go far enough. It is not sufficiently empirical. It takes both objects and interests in the large. Not *any* object, not *any* interest is relevant to the particular needs of the particular problem in this particular situation. If we are going to be empirical, let us be empirical. Take a concrete case. Never will any object of any interest be considered valuable in relation to this particular case. Some objects and some interests will be ruled out as ethically neutral. Others as relatively but definitely bad—disvalues. It is always *some* object of *some* interest which is discovered to have value in the concrete case. Otherwise, anything that we did in any particular situation, assuming that our behavior was interested, would be valuable. Which object and which interest in this concrete case is valuable depends upon their relation to the observable needs, and upon the consequences which the action taken to gratify this interest rather than that, brings in its train. Conflict of interests is always present in ethical situations. But "interests" must not be taken as an unanalyzed term.

The question of the conflict of "ultimate" ends of human conduct will not down. Surely, an empiricist must admit the existence of situations in which differences in evaluation seem to be unarbitrable. It is such situations that constitute impressive evidence for the view that moral judgments are "ultimately" arbitrary and subjective. For Dewey, however, judgments of this kind are ambiguous and incomplete. Certainly, there is a sense in which a liking or a preference may be called arbitrary. Although it has a cause, it has no reason, i.e., it does not express a judgment but is an organic event of attraction or aversion on all fours with any other organic event like a craving for sunlight or a taste for alligator pears. We do not speak of "ultimate conflicts" in tastes of food, although we recognize differences in tastes. Those who would reduce conflicts in value-judgments to brute differences in taste can never explain what the *value*-judgments are about. Nor what the conflict is about, since presumably the reference of my judgment of *fact* is "my taste" and of your judgment of fact, "your taste." The two judgments of fact do not contradict each other, for they are about two different things. But the two judgments of value do.

Where we speak of ultimate conflicts of value-judgment, Dewey would claim that our analysis is incomplete, that we either do not know or are unwilling to find out how these judgments are linked up with objective problems in a determinate context. It is this failure to relate value analysis to the objective problems and situations in which they are always found,

and to the modes of solution proposed by value-judgments, which is at the root of the tendency to multiply
"conflicts of ultimate ends" with such theoretical ease.
As a matter of plain experience, those who are actually arrayed in conflict rarely differ as far as their
verbal allegiance to ultimate ends is concerned. Everyone fights for "honor"; everyone strives for "happiness." If we were to stop short with their avowals, we
could never even determine whether there is a conflict of "ultimate ends." If we do not stop short with
avowals but link ends up with behavior, behavior with
problems, problems with social and historical contexts,
then we will see that what is called *the* ultimate end is
really being advanced as a method of dealing with certain objective needs and lacks in the situation. What
these needs and lacks are, is not always known, even
to those whose "ultimate" ends have grown out of them;
they have to be discovered in inquiry. When they are,
the consequences of acting on the proposed ultimate end
are related to the situation out of which they have developed. The whole process is one in which "the ultimate end" is tested. Where, if ever, do we stop? There
is a stopping point when the problem has been resolved,
just as there is a stopping point in the process of scientific verification when a certain set of observations is
regarded as sufficient to determine a solution of the
problem at hand. A problem may arise as to whether
the consequence of this method of dealing with the situation is satisfactory just as a problem may arise as to
whether this observation which confirms a hypothesis is
valid. But in both cases these are *new* problems. We are
not called upon to settle all problems at once.

It may be observed that Dewey assumes a predispo-

sition to submit judgments of value to the check of
inquiry, and that the willingness to do this already
presupposes a judgment of value. But is the situation
any different in scientific inquiry? Suppose a statement
of fact is made. An individual who makes it may be
unwilling to test it by the available methods of verification. He may even flatly refuse to do this. What follows? That *we* cannot characterize his statement as
true or false? Absurd. Similarly, we can evaluate, after
inquiry, the judgments of value of those who refuse to
engage in the process of inquiry, and reach an objective conclusion concerning their worth. In the course of
such an inquiry, we may even be able to discover, by
examining the situation, why they refuse to submit
their ends or standards—no matter how ultimate they
are declared to be—to further inquiry.

Finally, it may be asked: How do we know that conflicts of values can be resolved by the use of the experimental method? What assurance has Dewey that to
make *method* the source of authority will introduce
more order and agreement in our judgments of value
than the authority of state, church, or individual conscience? If assurance here means "guarantee," then the
answer is that Dewey has no assurance that the experimental method will resolve all conflicts in evaluation.
But the most pertinent answer we can give to this question is exactly like the response which we would make
to a comparable doubt in the field of science. How do
we know that any particular question of fact can be
settled by the use of scientific method? Having surrendered the quest for certainty, we can offer no guarantees. But in the domain of values as in the field of
natural science, we say: *Let us try the method out.* In

science the countless number of times that we have successfully used the experimental method makes its use
in any particular case reasonable. The fact that we
have used the experimental method so successfully in
the field of science, the fact that all other methods in
the field of morals have failed so disastrously, makes the
proposal to use it in the field of morals, at the very
least, not unreasonable. In the present state of the
world, perhaps it would not even be too much to say
that if we are to continue living together unaccursed
by war, poverty, and the remediable evils that flow
from them, the use of the experimental method is necessary.

In the light of the foregoing we may briefly review
some of the criticisms which have been passed on
Dewey's ethical theory before going on to his discussion
of means and ends. This will enable us to accent certain
features of his ideas which are often overlooked. The
interesting thing about these criticisms is the way they
cancel one another. This is due to the fact that although the two generic points of view—high apriorism
on the one hand, and subjectivism on the other—are
both ruled out by Dewey's theory, each one attributes
to him the systematic defects of the other. For one,
Dewey is not enough of a rationalist because he insists
that the meaning of values, ends, and standards is to be
found in human experience, in the interested behavior
of men in society. For the other, Dewey is too much of
a rationalist because he emphatically denies that an
irrational, unarbitrable liking confers moral quality
upon an act. According to Dewey, a moral principle

which flings its "ought" to the world irrespective of
what the world at any moment "is," which refuses to
have its ends roughhewn by the critical test of experimental living, mistakes personal caprice or the dead
weight of tradition for immutable first principles. In
the eyes of some, this makes his philosophy "opportun-
istic," "acquiescent," and "apologetic." But Dewey
has always maintained that no pattern of conduct in
any situation marked by doubt, crisis, or conflict should
be sanctioned merely by habit and use; value and justification depend upon what intelligence discloses about
the possibilities of improving that conduct. In the eyes
of others, this makes him a Utopian. Where Dewey
writes there are no standards or goods above criticism,
some read him as if he denied the existence or necessity
of any standards. Where he insists that ideals must
have a natural basis both in human need and the possibilities of the social order, some hear him say in substance, "Whatever is, is right." Where Dewey cautions:
Don't be too sure about your goal unless it can guide
you at least a little way ahead so that you can take
another reading—they complain: Dewey tells us how to
get ten steps ahead, but he does not tell us where and
what the goal is. As if the problem were not to determine what the goal should be! As if we could have a
genuine idea of *where* a goal was without it making
a difference to the steps taken to reach it! Where
Dewey urges that the needs at the heart of conflicting
moral demands be brought into the light in order to
discover to what extent they may be harmonized by
appropriate action, his method is damned as a technique of liberal compromise. Where he points out that
sometimes the appropriate action may involve a long

time change and basic alterations in a situation, he
frightens conservatives.

The common assumption behind all of these criticisms
is that there are intrinsic ends or values whose ethical
quality does not depend upon the means required to
achieve them. It is necessary therefore to consider in a
little more detail Dewey's theory of the continuity of
means and ends.

Ordinarily, when an individual is called upon to explain a particular action, he invokes some justifying
end. The end justifies the act as a means even if it
turns out that the means do not achieve the end. The
discussion about the adequacy of this or that particular
set of means is carried on with the end as a fixed point,
the assumption being that as far as the end is concerned it matters little what the means are. Out of this
attitude there develops the view expressed in the popular maxims: "The end justifies the means" or "The
end justifies the use of any means (provided only it is
successful)." Deliberation about the means is often considered as no part of an ethical action but rather a
mechanical task, more or less difficult, of carrying out
a decision already made, whose ethical validity is presupposed before concern with means begins. So much
presupposed that often someone else is entrusted with
the problem of finding the means, which appear as no
more than a detail—even if an important one—to those
who have framed the ends.

Yet the irresponsible character of such a procedure
lies at hand. After all, how do we know what a man's
"end" actually is? By what he tells us? Or by what he

sets out to do and the consequences of his doing? How do we know what our *own* ends really are? Words may come glibly in answer, but there are few who will not admit to uncertainty and irresolution until a process of deliberation has been completed. But what is there to deliberate about if the immediate quality of an end is its ethical justification? As soon as we begin to answer these questions, we see, says Dewey, that we do not know the meaning of an end without some notion of the means necessary to reach it. We cannot sincerely will an end, if we are intelligent, and not will the means required to bring it about. Only those who are wedded to an introspective psychology and a non-empirical theory of meaning can deny this.

When we ask: What means does any declared end commit us to? a number of things sometimes happen. We may find that the consequences of using the required means make impossible the existence of *other* ends which we had assumed to be compatible with the declared end. A man's fortune may be saved at the cost of his honor; the price of loyalty to an organization may be the surrender of intellectual integrity. "The end justifies the means" suddenly appears as equivalent to the belief that "this end justifies the sacrifice of all other ends," a type of fanaticism which borders on insanity. For normally human beings have irreducibly plural ends which they refuse to sacrifice on the altar of one great End. Unless we are supernaturalists, we can always ask the same kind of questions about the great End as about lesser ones.

Schematically, we may indicate the basic fallacy of the dictum that the end justifies the means as follows: We bring to every situation a set of ends or ideals which have established themselves as desirable because of previous reflective experience. Let us call them A, B, C, D, E. . . . By isolating one end A and invoking it to justify any means that will bring it about, or that promises to bring it about, we find that we are committed to doing b', c', d', e' . . . which violate our other ends or values B, C, D, E. . . . Since it is almost always the case that any one end is correlated with some other, which is violated when we act on the principle that anything is permissible by way of means, even the originally isolated sanctifying end A is rarely achieved in the form that had been anticipated. To a civilized person, no value is worth pursuing, no victory is worth winning, for which we are prepared to sacrifice all other values of experience.

In searching for means we may discover that our declared end is such that no available methods or means seem likely to achieve it. In that case we have a fancy or wish which, no matter how pleasing, does not relieve us of the responsibility for continuing the quest for an end that promises to give us some leverage in bringing it about. What is brought about we may call the end-in-fact; what we proclaim we want to bring about, we may call the end-in-view. In this world, what is actually brought about—the end-in-fact—does not depend upon the end-in-view, the declared goal, but is causally determined by the physical and social means employed to implement the end-in-view. The means and the consequences of the means are literally part of the end-in-fact. Insofar as we can foresee them, they are also part of the end-in-view. If we reaffirm an end-in-view in the light of the foreseen consequences of the means which seem to be integral with it, we have begun the process of criticism of our end. We have chosen intelligently, even if experience compels us to revise our conceptions of the required means or the desired end or both. In the course of action, means and ends act as checks upon each other in the same way as observational data and hypothesis function in relation to each other.

Utopianism consists in projecting an end-in-view without concern for the specific instrumentalities by which the end-in-view is to be embodied in an end-in-fact. Sectarianism consists in a dogmatic insistence that some one set of means necessarily must be adopted to reach the end-in-view independently of the empirical evidence available that the chosen set of means is ineffectual. Fanaticism is the ruthless effort to achieve a desired end-in-view by any means and at any cost to oneself and others. Opportunism in the pejorative sense is the use of the nearest means at hand that promises an easy advantage without reference to the end-in-view. Opportunism is sometimes the form taken by a frustrated fanaticism.

Dewey's theory of the continuity of means and ends has a very sharp cutting edge, as we shall later see, in the field of social philosophy. Here it is necessary to safeguard it against some typical misunderstandings. To say that means and ends mutually determine each other does not imply that at any two points in the process of moral action the same quality will be found. To dance with ease may be an end achievable only by the most rigorous training at the beginning. The buoyancy of good health may be attained only by a monotonous regime. The quality of the action at the outset and the finish differs, but the functional *relationship* between the end and the means at any two points in the process of activity is always the same when the action is intelligently executed. That is to say, the means are actually of a kind that lead to this end with greater economy than any other means available at the time; the end-in-fact, insofar as it is a consequence of the means used, is the end desired or the end-in-view.

Sometimes it is asserted that we undoubtedly approve of the end and disapprove of the means necessary to secure it. For example, all of us would like to have sound teeth, but certainly no one likes the painful drilling which is often necessary to get sound teeth. Is not the end good and the means bad? Here the confusion lies in identifying the immediate quality of liking or not liking with the judgment of approval or disapproval. In *any* course of action, approved or not, there are some parts we like (dislike) more than others. Pulling in the fish is more fun than digging for bait (if that is the only way we can get it). For some people, the preparation leading up to an event is more exciting than the consummation. But intelligent approval or disapproval has as its object not the isolated phases of an action in which the means are necessary to the end and vice versa, but the action as a whole, or that segment of the action which is relatively complete. In the illustration considered, I dislike the drilling as means and enjoy the sound teeth as a realized end. But it doesn't make sense, on any behavioristic view, to say I approve of sound teeth but disapprove of the drilling necessary to get it. I either approve or disapprove of the entire process. Any intelligent judgment made about it will take note of the varying qualities of the phases of the process as well as of all other relevant factors,

such as the expense and time involved, the consequences
of neglecting the treatment, etc.

May we not legitimately distinguish, it is sometimes
asked, between certain temporary or transitional means
of reaching an ultimate or permanent goal and the nature of a goal once achieved? The distinction lies in
differentiating between the merely instrumental—the
transitional means—which has no moral quality, and
the ultimate or permanent goal, which has. Of all the
vicious illusions that may be entertained about the relationship between means and ends, according to Dewey,
this is the most vicious. To begin with, the terms "transitional" and "ultimate" in this connection are completely question begging. Are the means "transitional,"
say, like the scaffolding of a building, or are they like
the elevators which, although used in the construction
of a building, remain a permanent part of it? More
important is the fact that the character of the goal
"ultimately" reached depends completely upon the character of the "transitional" instruments used. Not that
the aesthetic quality is the same, but rather that the
end actually achieved, the end-in-fact, is the result of
the whole series of "transitional" states which precede
it, *and nothing more*. The moral quality attaches to the
instruments or means as well as the end, to the transitional steps and to what eventuates from them. Usually
the insistence upon the distinction between transitional
periods and other periods from and to which they are
transitional, is motivated by a desire to enjoy a moral
holiday during a time period which is indefinitely elas-
tic. It is a demand made for unlimited credit in the
"benevolent" intentions of those who have power, intentions not subject to test by what is actually *done*

John Dewey

before everybody's eyes during the transitional period but which are presumably revealed in what those who have power *say*, and in the consoling myths and ideologies whose precise function is to discount the refuting evidence of experience.

The bearing of all this for a theory of social and political action hardly requires elaboration. All social ideals and philosophies which are not rhetorical devices to keep men in ignorance and subjection must be regarded as hypotheses or plans of action, and judged, like all other plans, by their consequences, their costs, and their achievements. How sharp the cutting edge of this approach is when applied to the tissue of present-day social problems we shall see in the next chapter.

Chapter

VIII

THE GOOD SOCIETY

IN one form or another all the classic figures in ancient and modern philosophy have been concerned with the nature of the good society. The perplexities, fears, and hopes of their time, and of the groups with which they associated themselves, enter even into metaphysical constructions whose speculative towers are lost in the sky. The task of tracing the influence of social problems, traditional allegiances, the pressures of political need and interest on abstract philosophic thought is rendered difficult by the apparent unconsciousness of most professional philosophers to the focal social questions of their age.

In John Dewey the concern with specific social problems and with the development of a social philosophy directly relevant to them is as clear as day. His starting point is empirical—the recognition of the existence of conflicts between groups, classes, nations, races, institutions. In approaching these conflicts he refuses to recognize any validity in the timeworn opposition between *the* social and *the* individual. His analysis of mind makes abundantly clear that to oppose the individual to society is to make an empty conceptual distinction. There is no mind, there is no individual, that measures itself as an independent entity over against society. Conflicts between individuals and groups of individuals there undoubtedly are and will be.

But every demand made in such a conflict has a social context, a meaning which already presupposes some form of associated behavior as something to be preserved or changed. A scientific social philosophy begins at the point where "considerations of definite conflicts, at particular times and places (are) substituted for a general opposition between social and individual."

The existence of social conflicts, if the community is to survive, requires an authority to settle conflicts. The easy opposition of freedom in the abstract to authority in the abstract is another illustration of defective social analysis. Historically, opposition to some specific oppressive authority has led to the exaltation of the principle of freedom as something absolute. In order to liberate themselves from a specific set of restraints, men have sometimes formulated a philosophy which, taken literally, would mean a freedom from all restraint. Every cry for freedom, however, has been a demand not merely to shake off restraints but for *power to do* certain things. Historically, the consequences of the freedom to do specific things have been such that a counterdemand for some authority to regulate and control action has arisen. The counterdemand in turn is overgeneralized. In order to secure themselves from the excesses of certain specific freedoms, men formulate principles which, again taken literally, would justify the surrender of all freedom. It is obvious that, despite the effectiveness of slogans which counterpose freedom and authority, they cannot be seriously taken as extrinsic to each other. There never was a society in which some authority was not operative. A period of social chaos or crisis cannot be defined as one in which authority is absent but rather as one in which there is a struggle between various authorities, the old and new, for domination.

There is authority and authority. Social conflicts may be settled by invoking a sacred dogma. They may be settled by appealing to a tradition, custom, or fixed law. They may be settled by ruthless exercise of force. Or by nonviolent but none the less effective forms of coercion, as in industrial disputes. Sometimes, when they do not cut too deep into vital social processes, they may not be settled at all. When we look around in the world today we find that social conflicts are by and large settled by forms of authority whose consequences are waste of natural and human resources, frustration of creative impulse, and intensification of material and psychological insecurity out of which the paranoic hates of fascism, brown, red, and black, develop.

The heart of Dewey's social philosophy is the proposal to substitute for the existing modes of social authority the authority of scientific method. Taken independently of Dewey's other doctrines, there is a bewildering simplicity about this proposal. It impresses some like an invitation to go prospecting for water while the house is burning. Others do not see even that much virtue in it. Scientific method as a means of resolving social conflict is not as effective as water in extinguishing fire; it is more like trying to put out raging flames by gently blowing on them. We shall try to determine what merit there is in these and similar objections after the complete argument is stated.

That scientific method is the only reliable source of authority in resolving conflicts of belief about the nature of the physical world, hardly anyone will doubt. Even those who are most vehement in denying the rele-

vance of scientific method to moral and social ends
admit that the question of the means by which ends are
to be effectively implemented is a scientific one. The
invalidity of the sharp separation between ends and
means has already been demonstrated in the previous
chapter, but we will not introduce its conclusions at this
point to cut the discussion short. It is also noteworthy
to observe that there is a whole group of social philosophies which do not deny, in theory, that *at some future
time* social conflicts will be resolved by scientific methods. What they do deny is that certain fundamental
conflicts *today* can be resolved scientifically. In relation
to these conflicts, they assert, Dewey's proposal is as
useless as the preachments of the philosophy of love.

The implications of the admission that scientific
method is relevant to means, and on the part of many
that in the future it will settle conflicts of ends (Dewey,
we shall see, is not so certain), are enormous. For
among the implications is a recognition of the fact that
at least in some sectors of experience, authority and
freedom do live in a happy and fruitful marriage. The
nature of scientific method is such that it allows full
freedom of inquiry to any individual, no matter what
his race, nationality, religion, or creed, and at the same
time, without any form of coercion, achieves an impressive agreement of belief through a set of common
conclusions that provides a further basis for free intellectual enterprise. We can hardly improve upon
Dewey's own statement of those features of scientific
inquiry which make it a working mode of the union of
freedom and authority:

"In spite of science's dependence for its development
upon the free initiative, invention and enterprise of

individual inquirers, the authority of science issues from and is based upon collective activity, cooperatively organized. Even when, temporarily, the ideas put forth by individuals have sharply diverged from received beliefs, the method used in science has been a public and open method which succeeded and could succeed only as it tended to produce agreement, unity of belief among all who labored in the same field. Every scientific inquirer, even when he deviates most widely from current ideas, depends upon methods and conclusions that are a common possession and not of private ownership, even though all the methods and conclusions may at some time have been initially the product of private invention. The contribution the scientific inquirer makes is collectively tested and developed. In the measure that it is cooperatively confirmed, it becomes a part of the common fund of the intellectual commonwealth."

That the extension of this method of authority to other areas of life is desirable, here and now, few would deny. That the obstacles to its introduction are formidable is also undeniable. For Dewey, the primary obstacles are institutional. By considering what they are we shall be able to understand those principles of Dewey's social philosophy which have a direct bearing upon the focal social and political questions of modern society. Afterward we shall examine the opposing contention that the very existence of conflicting interests *necessarily* rules out any possibility of organized intelligence—or the method of experiment—as the source of social authority.

The most obvious obstacle to the use of social intelligence on the widest scale is the existence of political

institutions which, by concentrating power in the hands
of a few, erect as a fixed end the interests of those who
control the strongest battalions. Freedom of social inquiry and the widest distribution of the results of such
inquiry cannot take place in a society where a group, a
class, a party, a church have a monopoly of political
power. It halts or rather is halted just at the point
where it threatens to expose, and therefore to weaken,
the holders of power. The widest use of organized intelligence is possible, therefore, only in a truly democratic society. *Possible* in such a society because it
provides greater opportunity for mutual consultation,
active participation by all adult minds affected by social policy, voluntary acceptance of checks and
controls—in short, institutional analogues of the scientific process. Dewey is careful *not* to suggest that
democratic societies as they are at present constituted
are the only ones in which science can flourish or that
scientific discoveries cannot be made in undemocratic
societies. After all, despite the mechanisms of democratic government, freedom of inquiry has often been
abridged; and the scientific renaissance in the Western
world began before the emergence of political democracy. What Dewey means is that the scientific temper
toward questions of social policy, and not merely toward questions of physical control, demands a democratic society for its fullest realization.

Why cannot authoritarian governments adopt a scientific approach to social policy? The assumption that
they can is often made by technocrats who believe in
government by engineers, and by "hard-boiled social
realists" who urge that since some form of minority rule
is inescapable anyhow, the rule of benevolent despots,

pictured as humane professional politicians or social psychiatrists, is the nearest we can come to good government. Some apologists of the totalitarian regimes of Hitler and Stalin have even defended the suppression of political democracy in Germany and Russia on the ground that its presence is incompatible with the four-year and five-year "experiments." Once these plans are begun, they argue, only traitors would experiment with the experiment: even in a laboratory a scientist would not permit anyone to tamper with his experiment before it was through.

What is overlooked in this position is the relation between the ends of social policy and the objective social needs which the policy is supposed to meet. An end may be carried out as scientifically as an execution and with the same consequences upon the bodies of the experimental victims. A scientifically chosen social end is one which promises to fulfill certain social needs. These needs are to be found in the living and cultural conditions of the individuals who constitute the community; and whether or not an adopted policy fulfills these needs can be determined only by those who are affected by this policy. There is good *scientific* warrant for the homely wisdom of the democrat that those who wear the shoe know best where it pinches. A scientifically chosen end, therefore, is one chosen by democratic concensus after free and public deliberation open to all whose needs set the problems for public policy. In the course of this deliberation it becomes clear which needs are to be met by the social experiment as well as their order of priority. A scientifically tested social experiment is one in which those who suffer its results for good or ill on their own bodies, not only have a share

in producing these results but in evaluating them. They
must also have the power to send the directors of the
experiment packing if they disapprove of the results.
To speak, then, of the German and Russian four- and
five-year plans as scientific experiments, when their
basic objectives were laid down by a minority group
within a minority party dictatorship, and submitted
for formal approval after every voice of opposition had
been stilled by *terror*—is to speak a bloody jest.

The second obstacle to the use of organized intelligence as a method of resolving conflicts so as to maxi-
mize the effective freedoms of individuals, is economic.
Where economic arrangements are such that they generate periodic and widespread insecurity and fear, give
men disproportionate power over other men by controlling the material means by which they live, produce
tensions and antagonisms between nations which burst
forth into conflagrations that threaten the whole structure of society—two pertinent conclusions may be
drawn. The first is that political democracy itself cannot long endure, and that even its existing forms must
work badly, so long as economic want is general. The
second is that in the light of available scientific knowledge and techniques there is not a shadow of justification for the systematic waste of men and materials and
the enforced restriction of production and consumption
which are indigenous features of capitalist economy.
The very facts that the fruits of scientific discovery
are applied to industry only insofar as they can justify themselves in terms of profit and war, that their
serviceability in gratifying genuine social needs is secondary, that it is possible to stake out a claim to
private and exclusive use of what has been won by the

methods of a common scientific heritage—are sufficient to condemn our economic system from the point of view of anyone who would take the rationale of scientific method as a guide to social practice.

It is now clear why, after a long study of the workings of the economic order, John Dewey believes that socialization of the basic instruments of production is necessary in the interest of organized intelligence. To establish the proper social conditions for the widest use of the experimental method, and for the effective freedom of all individuals to do socially productive work, requires more than the *ad hoc* palliatives of either the Old Deal or the New. It involves facing "the problem of remaking a profit system into a system conducted not just, as is sometimes said, in the interest of consumption, important as that is, but also in the interest of positive and enduring opportunity for productive and creative activity and all that that signifies for the development of the potentialities of human nature." The new liberalism for Dewey cannot stop with tacking on pieces of social legislation to an economy in the throes of crisis, measures which in other countries failed to stop the march of totalitarianism. "The cause of liberalism will be lost for a considerable period if it is not prepared to go further and socialize the forces of production, now at hand, so that the liberty of individuals will be supported by the very structure of economic organization."

This last quotation introduces an important theme in Dewey's social philosophy. For it indicates how strongly Dewey feels his continuity with the abiding, because ever-freshly established, values of freedom, individuality, and scientific enlightenment of the great liberal tradition in the Western world. It also indicates his awareness that a socialized economy which does not incorporate the methods of scientific inquiry and the forms of democratic process into the very fabric of social life will result in a new despotism, all the more monstrous because of the enormous power that can be wielded when the productive plant of a nation is rationalized.

It is impossible to understand the philosophy and crisis of liberalism except historically. In a masterly analysis of the social and political philosophy of liberalism in his *Liberalism and Social Action* (a book which may very well be to the twentieth century what Marx and Engels' *Communist Manifesto* was to the nineteenth), Dewey shows how the glorious ideals of early liberalism in relation to the specific historical conditions of the seventeenth to the nineteenth centuries, released personal and social forces from the restraints of a decaying feudalism without being able to supply an integrating philosophy for the new capitalist culture which had replaced it. The ideals of early liberalism were: freedom, "the development of the inherent capacities of individuals" made possible by freedom, and the sovereignty of "free intelligence in inquiry, discussion and expression." He shows further how the development of capitalist economy in effect frustrated these ideals. Their rhetorical shell became hypnotic catchwords to arrest further social development. In a powerful plea for a renascent liberalism, he argues that these ends can only be given concrete meaning and embodiment if they are understood in terms of the material means now at hand. If we are to escape from present and future regimentation of human beings, it must be by regimenting the mechanical and productive forces of society. "Organized social planning, put into effect for the creation of an order in which industry is socially directed in behalf of institutions that provide the material basis for cultural liberation and growth of individuals, is now the sole method by which liberalism can realize its professed aims."

It is not a planned society with fixed goals imposed from above which Dewey regards as the good society but a *"continuously planning"* society in which as much attention is given to preserving and extending civil and cultural liberties as increasing production norms. There is a planning for freedom as well as for plenty; and only the public recognition of the authority of scientific method in all spheres of conflict is competent to achieve it. The alternative to the social planning envisaged by Dewey is drift, increasing insecurity, and the only kind of planning so far perfected—planning for war. Dewey does not minimize in the slightest the hosts of difficulties which will attend every effort to control a unified economy. He is alive to important problems which no ideal of scientific planning can settle in advance, such as the degree of centralization or decentralization in industry, the relationship between private and co-operative farming, and the mechanisms of democratic control which must be worked out as safeguards against bureaucratic abuse of power. He does not attempt to solve these problems with a Utopian faith or a plausible formula but by an indication of what method to try if they are to be solved at all.

The demand then that the authority of scientific

method be recognized as the only effective agency in the
resolution of social conflicts is not as innocuous as it
seems. It points the way to a program of action in
behalf of a society whose basic economic structure is
markedly different from that of the present. It links
up the struggle for that program not with existing
forms of totalitarianism but with the liberating ideals
of American democracy. Accept for a moment with
John Dewey the supremacy of the method of inquiry in
resolving conflict, then you cannot escape accepting the
consequence he draws: "The objective precondition of
the complete and free use of the method of intelligence
is a society in which class interests that recoil from
social experimentation are abolished. It is incompatible
with every social and political philosophy and activity
and with every economic system which accepts the class
organization and vested class interest of present society."

This does *not* mean that the use of the method of
intelligence is to be postponed until a new social order
is instituted. The practices of some advocates of the
class struggle who profess to share the same "ultimate
ideals" of John Dewey would seem to support this fan-
tastic interpretation. For Dewey, the first task of intelligence is the discovery of the concrete means to
achieve the social ideal presupposed by its widest use.
The consideration of the means and their consequences
and of the alternative methods proposed to achieve the
social ideal enables us to test its validity. Theoretically,
although existing class society cripples the use of intelligence at many points, it may endure even a worse
fate in other social systems, especially if we note some
of the methods that are recommended to bring the lat-

ter about. To point to the evils of the existing order is therefore not enough. How do we know that the evils of the new order will not be even greater? That this is not an ungrounded fear is evidenced in what we can now observe in other parts of the world, particularly in Germany and Russia. At this point, we must briefly consider the relation of Dewey's social philosophy to the doctrines of socialism, anarchism, and communism.

The relation of experimentalism as a social philosophy to the revolutionary philosophies of the nineteenth and twentieth centuries is a question that has too many ramifications to be exhaustively treated here. A certain distinction must be made between the objective import of Dewey's statements, and Dewey's own consciousness of their import. As in the case of many other thinkers, the first usually takes us beyond the second. Here we wish to deal primarily with the social philosophy which Dewey himself is prepared to recognize as his own and not with its implications, no matter how reasonable, that would align him, if he were aware of them, with one or another political group. But even if we restrict ourselves to Dewey's own recognition of the bearing of his social philosophy, there is a further difficulty in the fact that Dewey's consciousness of his social philosophy has been enlarged. The turning point was the World War and its consequences. It requires no exegesis whatsoever to show that Dewey's present position is one that differs from democratic socialism only in name; nor was it merely as a gesture of protest that he actively campaigned for Norman Thomas in the last two presidential elections. Yet his implicit criticisms of the

revolutionary *systems* of thought and practice indicates that none of the conventional labels of left-wing
politics can be affixed to him. This is what we should
expect about anyone faithful to the spirit of the experimental philosophy.

In trying to understand why Dewey never embraced
the tenets of any of the conventional schools of radicalism, it should be borne in mind that he evaluated
them primarily as movements. It was as historical expressions, as forms which they took in the contemporary scenes of the last fifty years, that socialism,
anarchism, and communism were judged. He was never
moved to make an independent study of the theoretical
writings from which these movements draw their philosophy, their program, and even their tactical recipes.
He was quite content to accept on its face value the
genealogical tree which each movement offered of its
virtues and vices. Only someone educated in the family,
so to speak, is concerned with genealogical questions,
and Dewey, like most Americans of his time, was reared
differently. Consequently Marxism for Dewey was what
those who called themselves Marxists made of it; just
as Marxists would say that Christianity is what those
who call themselves Christians live by.

Socialism, as Dewey knew it in its prewar days, was
a movement with whose critique of the evils of capitalism he was sympathetic. But he could never accept the
set of dogmatic beliefs about history, man, and the inevitable course of social development which accompanied it. A crude economic determinism, together with a
prediction of a literal economic collapse, were applied
in a wholesale and unqualified fashion to all events.
There was no differential analysis of specific happen-

ings, no balancing of probabilities about future oc-
currences, no adequate recognition of the role of human
beings in bringing them about. In practice, despite its
strenuous avowals of ultimate revolutionary aims, prewar socialism (Social Democracy) was reformist in
character. Although heartily in favor of most of these
reforms, Dewey believed they could be more effectively
embodied by a native "progressive" movement free from
dogmas about a great historical apocalypse, and continuous with American liberal tradition.

The communist movement which took shape after the
War had even less to recommend it. In Dewey's eyes it
made a fetishism of the conquest of political power,
ostensibly in the name of a class, actually in behalf of
a dictatorial group of "professional revolutionists." In
its struggle for power, it resorted to means which were
better adapted to produce the opposite of its alleged
goals than anything else. In its twists and turns of
policy which ranged from an outright call to insurrection by force of arms to a silly posturing of super-
Americanism, and even to a public denial, whenever it
was deemed opportune, of its own creed, he saw reflected
the foreign policy of the Kremlin, not genuine concern
for the needs of the American people. His own experience with communists in the fields of labor, education,
and civil liberties convinced him that save for certain
irrelevant phraseological differences, their behavior was
hardly distinguishable from that of their socially identical twins—the Fascists and Nazis.

Anarchism, as a belief in propaganda by the deed, he
regarded as a form of social pathology. Anarchism as
a belief in a society without any authority, he rejected
as a romantic illusion. With anarchism as a faith in

the capacity of human beings to settle their differences
without coercion, he was more sympathetic. But he
interpreted this as a directive to use intelligence as a
method of social reconstruction and authority so as to
reduce the amount of coercion in the affairs of men,
not as an absolute faith in a natural goodness of man
uncorrupted by social arrangements.

In all of the different revolutionary isms, even when
he admired the courage and selfishness of some of their
proponents, he was repelled by a fierce monism which
clung to fixed ends as if they were the keys to heaven;
by the uncritical tendency to generalize the means of
implementing ends independently of specific, historical
contexts; by rapid shifts from fanatical and ineffectual
sectarianism to unprincipled opportunism.

In two respects, however, Dewey did learn from the
socialist movement. Despite the overemphasis on the
controlling nature of economic conditions, its perception of the social and economic forces operating to
bring the United States into the World War was empirically more accurate than Dewey's. On the basis of
his experience of what happened to the democratic war
aims of 1917, Dewey has become one of the most outstanding advocates of an American antiwar policy in
the present-day crisis of Western civilization. Despite
its benefit of theory, international socialism failed to
prevent the World War or even, like Dewey, to oppose
it. But at least it knew what the War was about. The
second respect in which Dewey learned from the
socialist movement was that under present conditions experimental tinkering with money, credit, tariff, regulation of monopoly, etc., was not sufficiently fundamental
to gratify the needs for security, employment, and a

decent standard of living for all Americans. " 'Reforms' which deal now with this abuse and now with that without having a social goal based upon an inclusive plan, differ entirely from reforming, in its literal sense, the institutional scheme of things." This is part of the wisdom of socialism and strikes a note quite different from what one hears in his earlier political writings. For the greater part of his life he was convinced by the evidence supplied by an expanding capitalism that its basic evils could be eliminated by traditional progressivism. In 1929, however, *before* the depression broke, in a series of prescient articles, Dewey made the great turn. The diagnosis of the socialists was admitted to be justified. Dewey had reached it by piecemeal analysis without waiting for the economic crash which drove so many unintelligent intellectuals, out of fear, to the ideological bomb shelters of a new doctrinal security, accepted as naïvely as the ones from which they had just fled.

As far as the literature on the subject goes, the chief criticism of Dewey made from the point of view of his socialist critics is his underestimation of the necessity of the class struggle as *the* means of achieving the social order presupposed by the untrammeled use of the method of intelligence.

Only those who have not read Dewey can assert that he ignores the existence of class struggles in modern society. His emphasis, however, is upon class struggles in their *plural* form. Except on the basis of an arbitrary definition, we must recognize struggles not only between capitalist and worker but between capitalist and capitalist, workers and workers, farmers, unemployed, etc. The existence of these struggles indicates the existence of certain needs, lack, and wants in the living conditions of the great masses of producers and consumers. Insofar as class struggles are intelligently conducted, they must aim not only at improvement of conditions which have become intolerable but at the elimination of those institutional features of the economy which are obstacles to the continuous improvement of living conditions made possible by modern technology. The real question, then, is not whether class struggles exist or whether these struggles are to become the instruments of their own elimination but rather *how they are to be conducted.* And here Dewey maintains that it is a great error to assume that class struggles must of necessity be of a violent character, that they necessarily must burst through the forms of the democratic process or inevitably develop into civil war, or that there is such a thing as *"the* law of the class struggle" which gives a blanket justification to *any* method of beating an opponent. He denies that all great social changes of the past have been effected only by violent upheavals and argues that even if it were so in the past this does not by itself rule out the possibility of successful nonviolent action in the present.

The method of intelligence must investigate the evidence at hand in the present. After all, everyone admits that changes accomplished peacefully, even if noisily, are preferable to changes wrought by violence. Violence is only justified when it is used to stop or head off the danger of greater violence. The destruction loosed by a civil war in a highly technological society may be so extensive that a common ruin may befall all contending parties. For these and other reasons, Dewey affirms that only a dogmatic unintelligence will prejudge the question in advance and forego the attempt to broaden and use the actual mechanisms of political democracy to introduce social change. A fixed belief in the *inevitability* of violence is an illustration of such dogmatic unintelligence and contributes to bringing about the state of affairs which it later uses as an *ex post facto* justification for its own acts of violence.

The experimental method applied to the problem of bringing about the objective social conditions for its widest use is not to be identified with the method of sweet and ineffectual reasonableness, as its political detractors assert. There are other alternatives to sweet and ineffectual reasonableness than espousal of the inevitability of ruthless civil war. Those who justify the latter on the ground that it is a necessary form of social surgery blind themselves by a defective and presumptuous analogy. They assume that we have comparable scientific knowledge in deciding when surgery is necessary; they forget that a surgical operation is performed in civilized societies only with the freely given consent of the patient or his guardians; they blithely assume that they will be the surgeons and not the victims of the surgery. What the alternatives are depends upon a study—a difficult but imperative study —of each historical situation. "As far as experience and reflection indicate that pacific measures are most likely to be effective, the (experimental) philosophy is pacifist; where the reverse is indicated by the best available knowledge of actual conditions, it is revolutionary."

Insofar as the argument from recent history is relevant, Dewey claims that it is on his side, not on the side of his revolutionary critics. For in every country

of the world their methods have failed, and in the one
country in the world where they have taken power, the
results have been a ghastly travesty of socialist ideals.
The simple fact is that we have less knowledge about
the effective methods of achieving political consent and
power than we imagine. This calls not for retreat into
acquiescence or for desperate adventures but for an
intelligent action that explores every promising avenue
of co-operation and struggle, and learns from experience. Dewey himself has learned from experience. He
gave up his belief that the major political parties could
be weaned away from their allegiance to capitalism. In
the light of the N.R.A. and the New Deal, he has
abandoned his belief that the objective needs of the
American people can be adequately fulfilled by a "co-
ordinating and directing council" of representatives of
big business, government officials, and labor leaders.
This suggestion, made by Dewey in 1929, became the
basis of the first New Deal. In action it resulted in
making the strong stronger and the weak weaker.
Today Dewey believes that independent political action
by an alliance of all workers, farmers, and members of
the professions is the first step in the democratic march
to power necessary to introduce long-overdue social
changes.

The discussion of the ways and means of implementing a social program is so often carried on in the hectic
atmosphere of factional controversy that participants
are more interested in refuting a position than in understanding it. There is no other explanation of the
attempts that have been made to portray Dewey as a

pacifist and, when this does not stand up, as one who
would lame militant struggle for a better world by invoking "eternal principles of morality." These two
points must be considered separately.

If pacifism is a doctrine which makes a fetish of
nonresistance or passive resistance at all times and at
any price, then it follows at once from his ethical theory
that he cannot be a pacifist. But he refuses to grant
that the only alternative to pacifism is "putchism" or
minority insurrection in behalf of "good causes." There
are situations in history in which revolutions are justified. As an American democrat, he could not consistently be opposed to all revolutions without repudiating
the American Revolution, in whose fire the American
nation was forged. He believes, however, that existing
democratic processes in America, as defective as they
are in certain respects, make it possible to win over a
majority of the people to a program of basic socialization. He does not believe in imposing such a program
on the nation by force; nor even in the attempt to
carry it out behind the backs of the electorate, as some
"political realists" have proposed, by substituting it
for some other program on which confidence has originally been won. He insists that the issue be put squarely
before the people as a whole and is content to abide by
any decision made in any situation in which there is no
monopoly of political power or propaganda. Nothing
short of this can satisfy any sincere democrat.

In his *Liberalism and Social Action,* Dewey reminds
his revolutionary critics that both Marx and Engels
maintained that in England and America the program
of socialization could be achieved peacefully through
normal democratic processes. Once, however, a majority

mandate has been secured for such a program, any effort to nullify it by force should be sternly met by force. Otherwise the community would be at the mercy of any resolute minority of armed men. Together with Marx, Dewey believes that in America things need not come to such a pass. He is prepared to go a long way to placate, compromise with, and even buy off a recalcitrant minority, on the ground that it is cheaper than civil war. He is hopeful about the possibility that America can make a peaceful transition to a socialized economy.

It is hard to see how anyone except a fanatic can fail to share in Dewey's gallant hope. The only point at which criticism is legitimate is in his evaluation of the probabilities. The differences reduce themselves to an issue of *fact*. Will the overlords of American industrial and financial life accept a democratically arrived-at decision? Or will they attempt or abet a "proslavery" rebellion? No matter how one answers these questions, since we cannot be sure one way or the other and since so much depends upon it, it is a necessary part of political wisdom to be prepared for every eventuality. In the light of recent events in Europe, even in the light of American history, there does not seem to be much ground for optimism. But at any rate the majority must safeguard itself against being taken unawares, and organize its power to a point where potential insurrectionists would be discouraged. Dewey would be the first to admit that it is intelligent to be prepared and that there is no reason why those who believe in democracy should be unintelligent. Those who tax him with pacifism really take issue with his acceptance of the democratic process.

If Dewey is no pacifist, he is still less "a professional revolutionist" prepared to resort to *any* means that will further the transfer of power from one group to another. The "professional revolutionist" may speak of democracy, freedom, peace, security; but these are admittedly agitational slogans, scheduled to be discarded as soon as they threaten to limit the power of the self-appointed guardians of the revolution.

In a very interesting analysis Dewey has laid bare the methodological fallacy of every political doctrine which proclaims that "the welfare of the revolution is the supreme law" or, as it is sometimes put, "revolutionary necessity knows no law." The best representatives of this position begin with a declaration with which few would differ. They assert that morally anything is justified which "increases man's power over nature and decreases man's power over man." It is then argued that these ends can most effectively be furthered by a change in the relations of production which defines the content of a social revolution. But they couple with this doctrine another, according to which it is "*the* law of *the* class struggle" which determines the means that are to be employed to bring about a revolution and to preserve it. When a concrete case arises, by shifting from the first position to the second, the responsibility for the means used in the struggle is thrust on an alleged "law" working itself out inevitably to a revolutionary victory. Instead of presenting concrete evidence that any particular set of means does *in fact* lead "to the increase of man's power over nature and the decrease of man's power over man," *the* law of *the* class struggle is invoked as a blanket justification for the use of any means. At most it is argued that these means will lead to "our victory." This may be granted, but whether a victory achieved by *these* means will in fact further the ends-in-view instead of their opposite—that is the question! It is a question that Dewey believes can be decided only by intelligent analysis in each historical situation, not by appealing to an unanalyzed dogma of *the* class struggle nor by falling back on "eternal principles of morality" whatever they are.

It is a form of metaphysical mysticism or arrogant conceit or both to argue that any means that will give "us" victory necessarily will lead to a better society. Means are more significant, even if less eloquent, than intentions; and it is the quality of institutions rather than the quality of the personality of a leader which basically determines the weal or woe of a people.

Will the method of intelligence succeed in resolving conflicts in any society where other methods have failed? Dewey does not answer with a categorical affirmative. In view of the failure and cost of other methods, he urges that the least we can do is to try it out. There are others, however, who answer the question categorically in the negative. The method of intelligence *must* fail, they assert because conflicts of interests are not arbitrable on scientific grounds. The very existence of interests means that no rational adjustment of interests is possible. For interests are not truth-claims but forms of psychological and economic power. Let us listen to the criticism of Reinhold Niebuhr on the "pathos" of Dewey's liberalism: "It does not recognize the relation of social and economic inter-

est to the play of intelligence upon social problems. It
does not perceive the perennial and inevitable character
of the subordination of reason to interest in the social
struggle. Its ideal of a 'freed intelligence' expects a
degree of rational freedom from the particular interests
and perspectives of those who think about social problems, which is incompatible with the very constitution
of human nature."

Far from failing to recognize the relation of interest
to the play of intelligence upon social problems, Dewey
defines social problems in terms of conflicts of interest.
Since thinking to a purpose always refers to a problem, thinking about social problems cannot escape
concern with interests. To speak of "the inevitable subordination of reason to interest in the social struggle"
is to assume both that everybody already knows what
his genuine interests are before subjecting them to
critical analysis, and that no conflict of interests has
ever been reasonably adjusted. Indeed Niebuhr's position proves too much. If it is part of "the very constitution of human nature" to subordinate all conceptions
of the reasonable to a brutely given interest, itself not
subject to evaluation, *all* social policies are equally
arbitrary. Niebuhr's own social program, then, would
have no more objective validity than that of Hitler's
or Stalin's which he condemns. But he denies that his
espousal of it as "better" is only another way of saying
that it is his. Certainly, where conflicts of interest *are*
irreducible there is no alternative but to compromise or
fight just as men must do when they face tigers and
mad dogs. But how do we know in advance of reflective
analysis that the basic needs of men are so utterly
different that any set of conflicting interests are

irreducible? How do we know that no institutional arrangements are possible which will provide for the gratification of some inclusive set of social interests? How do we know in advance that in the light of these inclusive social interests the different interests in original conflict may not be modified to a point where the conflicts but not the differences disappear? Niebuhr knows all this in advance because he knows in advance what "the very constitution of human nature" is. The unalterability of human nature once more! Pull out this false psychological prop and the argument collapses.

The Utopian Marxist believes that once present class conflicts are eliminated, the future will be like heaven where everyone sings according to his capacity and is measured for a harp and halo according to his need. The realistic Marxist believes that once production is democratically socialized, future conflicts between men are more likely to be settled without the bloody struggles that are a feature of present-day culture. Dewey here is much closer to the realistic Marxist than Niebuhr. (Marxism is *not* present-day Communism; nor is it Bolshevik-Leninism.) Leaving aside certain secondary differences of terminology, it seems to me that, were realistic Marxists prepared to submit their methods of achieving *democratic* socialism to serious scientific criticism, and were Dewey prepared to work out a more detailed program of political action with reference to the social and economic relations of the current scene, their positions would converge on a set of common hypotheses leading to common activities.

There remains the question of the sense in which we can speak of a social "experiment." One can have cheap sport with the ideal of social experimentation by imagining that an experiment in social affairs is to be conducted like an experiment in a laboratory. In many fields of study ranging from astronomy to geology to the historical disciplines, it is possible to reach scientific conclusions, even though it is impossible to establish the controlled variation of the laboratory experiment. The experimental method in social affairs is present wherever a critical use is made of the method of agreement and difference. Since the subject matter of the social sciences is different from that of the physical sciences and enormously more complex, it is necessary to work out special techniques of observation, and to content oneself with a relevant degree of probability as far as conclusions are concerned. But the logic of inquiry is the same.

Dewey's proposal is that we regard every social policy as a plan or hypothesis to be tested by observable consequences which bear on the problem we have set out to solve. Which plan or hypothesis to put to a test is to be determined not by an edict of a pope, or Führer, or Beloved Leader, but only by the deliberative processes of a democratic society. Whether the policy has been successful is again to be determined by the reports of those members of the community who are affected by the results of the experiment. Provided the experimental planning is carried on within the framework of a democratic society, there is no objection to the fact that systematic control of certain aspects of the behavior of all individuals in the community for a limited period is instituted. Cut Dewey's advocacy of the method of experiment out of its democratic context, as some sly apologists of totalitarianism have done, and you then get the suggestion that what Dewey is proposing is that human beings be treated like rats in a maze for the benefit of an experimental psychologist.

Already in some fields of personal relationship a beginning has been made in the use of the experimental method to remove some obstructions to the effective functioning of men and women in relation to their social environment. Since Dewey believes that the gravest obstructions to the development of integrated personalities flow from deficiencies in the institutions which constitute their environment, he proposes to extend the experimental method to the field of *social* relationships. The willingness to undertake the task, the risk, and the high adventure of building an experimental and experimenting democracy, depends in part upon the habits of thought and action, which it is the function of education to develop. It is therefore not surprising that Dewey's social philosophy is also a philosophy of education.

Chapter

IX

THE FRONTIERS OF EDUCATION

AS every informed person knows, John Dewey's philosophy has borne its most immediate practical fruits in the field of education. His ideas have marched into the classrooms of public and private schools, even into the offices of administrators, and profoundly transformed the formal educational environment of millions of students and teachers. No matter what the nature of future educational theory will be, it is extremely unlikely that educational practice will ever return to the state it was in before John Dewey's influence made itself felt on the schools of the nation.

As important as that influence has been—and no recent theoretical influence has been more important—it has been limited. Limited by the way it has been interpreted, limited by the way it has been applied, limited by the absence of certain social conditions whose existence its ideals presupposed—and limited, above all, in comparison with the tremendous possibilities of educational reconstruction which would follow from a nationwide experiment in carrying out its basic principles.

It is understandable that professional educators should be primarily attentive to the immediate uses of an educational philosophy rather than to its fundamental ideas and values, in short, to the very things which make it a philosophy. But over a span of years,

177

unfamiliarity or unconcern with philosophic assumptions that are not directly relevant to day-by-day practice is sure to be costly to the educational technician. Historical situations change, the practices of yesterday become inadequate, new emphasis and adjustments must be made. Without a grasp of philosophical principles and an insight into the logic of scientific method, the teacher who has merely adopted the most conspicuous applications of an educational theory becomes bewildered. His bewilderment grows deeper when he is confronted by new (and old) philosophies of education, that always emerge in troubled times, which direct their attack against the theory of education whose conclusions he has accepted without understanding on what leading philosophic ideas they are based, and how they are derived. Of no philosophy of education is it truer than of Dewey's that its relevant import can be grasped only in the light of its ideas of knowledge, mind, human nature, experience, value, and democracy. As we shall see, Dewey's philosophy of education is not a philosophy merely for the professional educator. Although it is the educator who must be most sensitive to its implications for formal education, it is a philosophy for every intelligent member of the community. For it is a philosophy of life—bearing directly on our current moral, social, and political problems.

In this chapter, Dewey's leading educational ideas will be stated and their incidence traced upon latter-day educational issues which have arisen since the time they were originally formulated.

Education is as broad as the transmission of culture. It takes place whenever techniques, values, attitudes, bodies of knowledge are passed on from individual to individual or generation to generation. Schooling is only one mode of education and arises comparatively late in the development of human culture. Today, however, as a result of the complexities in the division of labor, the school is the most important single agency of formal education. Its general tasks are to provide a controlled special environment in which the capacities of the young are developed; to build up certain attitudes, sentiments, and loyalties, regarded as socially desirable, into habitual responses; and to give instruction in a miscellaneous variety of knowledge considered relevant to the present and future needs of those who receive it.

Education is a process in which present experiences are so directed that their results make future experiences more accessible to us. By perception of the meanings of our activities in meeting the problems of present experience, our powers of understanding and control of future experiences are enhanced. The end of education is to produce educated men and women where "educated" means to be in possession of trained power to meet and master the inescapably fresh experiences of living. This power is marked by the presence of sensitivity, resourcefulness, and command of skills and materials. Its functions are to enrich the qualities of immediate experience and to prevent habits from becoming immobilized in deadening routines. The end of education, then, is growth accomplished by means which themselves mark growth. "The educative process is a continuous process of growth, having as its aim at every stage an added capacity of growth." Insofar as individuals are different from each other, the educational process should provide possibilities for individualized growth. At the same time it should make available, as the basis of such growth, the common knowledge, disciplines, and techniques which are part of our collective cultural heritage and which are necessary not merely for growth but for sheer survival wherever individuals live together.

The misunderstandings which dog Dewey's ethical theory arise here, too. Just as it was asked: What is *the* good? so it is again asked: What is *the* end or *the* direction of growth? His answer is of a piece in one field as in another. The process and method of constructing *goods* is the only thing that can be called *the* good; the process of growth which produces whole clusters of values, personal and social, from phase to phase, and which at the same time creates the condition for *further* growth, is the only thing that can be called *the* end of growth.

If education aims to make the activities and results of present experience instruments of control over future experience, it follows that its relation to social institutions, social conditions, and problems, which obviously affect the occasions of both present and future experience, is as intimate as the relation between morals and society. This relationship is such that every educational philosophy is at the same time a social philosophy, and conversely. We can, therefore, use our educational philosophy directly as a criterion for evaluating any given set of social arrangements. Does a given social order make possible the achievement of growth for all the individuals educated within it? Does it liberate and at the same time integrate the intellectual, aesthetic, imaginative capacities of the young? Dewey would judge a society by its schools and by the effects of their schooling. But not only by its schools. If we remember that education as a process does not stop with the end of formal schooling, then it will be clear that it is not merely what goes on in the classroom but also what goes on in mine, field, and factory which must be evaluated in its bearing on the growth of the mind, character, and capacities of individuals. This philosophy of education may lack rhetorical ornateness but it has a tremendous impact upon the existing educational and social scene. Coupled with relevant knowledge, it leads to perfectly concrete proposals for social action. For, if it is in earnest about removing the obstructions to the realization of the educational ideals of growth, its attention is necessarily directed to an examination of the social facts which determine whether these ideals are to remain pious resolutions or whether they are to find a grip or leverage in changing situations.

We have space to discuss only the most daring and far-reaching of the social corollaries of Dewey's educational philosophy. Growth is the end of the educational process. All growth is pre-eminently an affair of interaction, and on the educational level the interaction is primarily social. The social contexts in which trained capacities, natural inclinations, and the needs of the community can best reinforce each other are provided by vocations, callings, careers—that is, by what people do to earn their living. Schooling whose end is growth is under the obligation of discovering for each individual what social career would bring into play and

fruitful use the powers he has grown into. A society
whose schools have this function is under the obligation
of so organizing its institutions that the discoveries of
the schools can be given social effect. It is not in the
interests of narrow vocational efficiency, or of trade
and business needs, that the walls between school and
society must be leveled but in order that the promise
and ideals of education for growth be fulfilled. To
grow, and to function as one has grown, demands the
presence of social opportunities to grow as well as an
environment in which to continue growing by doing.
Where the schools cannot influence the distribution of
available careers so that they go to those best qualified
for them, the result is frustration of growth. There is
something grotesque about nurturing skilled mechanics,
musicians, engineers, scholars, and other trained individuals to maturity and then leaving it to the chances
of the market or of government relief whether they
find employment at all, not to speak of the kind of employment. When the school is considered a part of the
educational process, and not the whole of it, a part
which feeds into and is fed by other institutional activities, all considered as different sectors of one unending
educational front, then and only then will the opposition between "earning one's living" and "living one's
life" disappear. This interpenetration of school and
community cannot be achieved in a caste society, nor
where there are fixed economic or hereditary divisions.
Its obvious presupposition is a democratically planned
and planning society.

Intelligence is a central value, and training for intelligence a central activity, in any educational scheme
which aims at maximizing possibilities of growth. For

what other instrument is more effective in enabling us to discriminate between experiences, to discern aspects of old experience which are relevant to the new, and to order experiences in such a way that they will be diversified without being anarchic? Intelligence in education, therefore, like growth itself, is a product and a process, an end and means. It is a mode of experience whose consequences enrich the qualities of all other experiences.

The immense fertility of these ideas is manifest in the concrete measures and practices which have sprung up on every level of school life from kindergarten to university in the last generation in the name of "the new" or "progressive" education. The adjectives are sometimes misleading, and Dewey has evinced no fondness for them. But the leading ideas which inform them are his. These are simple, few, but not easy of application. The goals and objectives of education should be set by the interest, capacities, and range of life experience of the developing child; they should not be imposed by adults as fixed ends, nor the educational life of the young considered as one long preparation for them. The subject matter and materials of education should be drawn from the present environment, and from whatever sources of the past that are *relevant* to the present; they should not consist of predigested matter in textbooks. The methods of education should evoke directed activity, experiment, and personal inquiry to test principles and results; not mechanical drill in skills and techniques which usually are not even plausibly motivated. The spirit of the classroom should be that of a group of co-operating individuals rather than that of a miniature Führer at whose commands well-trained martinets move with silent precision.

Despite its own grave shortcomings in interpretation and practice, progressive education has revealed the inadequacy of the formal stereotypes of traditional education. Even its critics dare not openly suggest as an alternative a return to the older practices—except when they run so far back to the past that they smack of novelty. It is the existing state of progressive education, then, which should be taken as the point of departure for further advance and correction. Despite the ideals of progressive education, correction is very much needed. Confusion abounds partly as a result of the economic consequences of declining capitalism, which have forced retrenchment in plant and personnel where expansion is in order; partly as a result of the emergence of totalitarian political philosophies which promise short cuts to an ideal education in the *future;* and not least because of the failure of the practitioners of progressive education to realize that organization, authority, and discipline can serve the purposes of freedom and growth. The weaknesses of progressive education are dangerous to the extent that they prepare the uncritical minded for modern versions of authoritarianism and fundamentalism whose cures spell the death of democracy and freedom of inquiry.

The root of many of the errors in modern progressive education is a tendency to substitute improvisation for experiment. Just as some people imagine that to evaluate standards critically is to abandon all standards, so they believe that the refusal to fix a rigid curriculum for all children means no organized curriculum for any children. Actually, as Dewey repeatedly warns, the new education is more difficult to carry out, requires more planning, more self-imposed discipline, more intelligent leadership on the part of teachers than the old. Here, as in every other phase of experience, the problem is to meet an immediate need in such a way that meeting it establishes a principle that may fruitfully be extended to other needs. Experiences have common features, even when their qualities are individualized. To try to do justice to the present needs of the child without losing sight of the needs of the community in which he now lives and is going to live, to develop individual personality free of egomania, to evoke initiative without the desire for domination, and co-operativeness without servility, cannot be accomplished by making a fetish of unrestrained self-expression. Children must be introduced under skillful guidance into situations where effective participation depends upon the recognition of the rules, the discipline, and the controls which flow from the nature of the subject matter itself and from the character of their associated activity. Authority is indispensable, but in the last analysis it must follow from the *method* of getting things done with the best results, the least friction, and the most joy.

Granted that progressive education can get "better," can it ever become "good enough" in a society which falls so far short of a good society? Are not all efforts to improve the quality of the educational process doomed to fail where the social presuppositions are lacking to make "growth" a directive ideal rather than a pious wish? Is not Dewey's position that school and

society inseparably reflect each other self-defeating if
he believes that either one can be used to improve the
other? The good society cannot come into existence
without the good education: the good education is possible only in a good society. But both cannot come
into existence at once except as a miracle out of the
blue. Can education, then, conceived in the spirit of
Dewey's philosophy, develop any other kind of individuals but precious misfits?

These questions are important because out of them
has arisen the belief that indoctrination for desirable
social change is a legitimate, and even necessary, part
of education. Existing educational practices in many
respects show a systematic bias which indoctrinates for
the social *status quo*. It is not enough to undermine this
bias, some say, it must be replaced by a new bias which
will indoctrinate students with a militant zeal to
bring into existence the new society which is presupposed by the new education. Among educators who
have adopted this position will be found some who have
been influenced by Dewey and who have urged it upon
him as a necessary complement to his philosophy.

Underlying the questions asked above is the assumption that we must commit ourselves either to the view
that education can do everything or that it can do
nothing in changing society. Dewey as usual cuts under
this false disjunction. We start from where we are. We
can do something. It is not true that all educational
efforts are necessarily doomed to failure. Even if they
fail, they are not worthless. The forces that influence
social development are many, and education is only one
among them. As educators, we cannot indoctrinate for
a society which is to be free from indoctrination with-

out becoming victims of the ethical fallacy that the end
justifies the use of any effective means, and of the educational fallacy that the present is to be considered
only as a preparation for the future.

Indoctrination is a method of protecting something
which, it is feared, cannot survive criticism. Indoctrination as a method of education is indispensable in
societies in which the source of authority is some vested
interest which would be weakened were it exposed to
analysis or compelled to compete with alternative modes
of authority. Even naked power feels more secure when
it can dress itself up in some semblance of doctrine to
cloak its oppressions. Indoctrination is a process in
which all the psychological techniques of iteration, association, substitute stimuli, and the conditioned reflex
are employed to produce habits, attitudes, and beliefs
that cannot be justified by an examination of their consequences or by other relevant evidence. Indoctrination
always serves some presumed good itself not subject to
criticism. How, then, can a philosophy which reposes
authority on matters of belief only in the methods of
scientific inquiry resort to indoctrination without gross
contradiction and insincerity? If its conclusions are
sound, they can be reached on the evidence. Of all the
misconceptions about the nature of the experimental
method, none is so curious as the notion that it cannot
lead to conclusions, decisions, or resolute convictions.
On the contrary, "it trusts to convictions which are
firm because confirmed in experience rather than those
which are intense mainly because of immaturity." If
judgment on some points has to be suspended it is not
because the method followed is unreliable but because
of the state of the subject matter under investigation.

It is sometimes objected that the experimental or scientific method can vouchsafe conclusions only about the world of nature, not about the social world, where the basic issues revolve around questions of policy. But, as we have already seen in the previous chapters, one of the great merits of Dewey's ethical theory is that it shows that problems of valuation, which lie at the heart of all social policy, are *in principle* arbitrable by the same generic pattern of inquiry as conflicting beliefs about anything else.

It is not necessary, therefore, for one who accepts the superior validity of democracy or scientific method to indoctrinate in their behalf. He need not have any fear of the outcome if he presents them in conjunction with their alternatives and considers the history of their respective uses. As distinct from their rivals, democracy and scientific method are self-critical. Far from fearing the test of argument and evidence, they invite it, something which none of their substitutes can afford to do. The greater danger is that in indoctrinating for democracy, as some of its defenders are now urging, the principle will be identified with a particular set of institutions which express it very imperfectly. Criticism of these institutions will then be construed as an attack on the principle itself. The *continuous* quest for improvement in material and ideal culture, and the *unceasing* crusade to establish safeguards against power-loving bureaucrats, *both* of which are parts of the democratic way of life, would soon be brought to a halt.

Just as, in politics, the democratic principle itself should be the guide to the actions which make society more democratic, so the critical methods of education should be the means of making individuals more intelligent. Nowhere does Dewey assert that the schools can change or rebuild society or that this falls directly in their province. The occasions on which choices must be made whose consequences radically affect society are not of the kind in which teachers, or any one generation of students, play a preponderant role. The *willingness* to consider choices, the strength to escape from the hypnosis of the established, the sobriety to assay glittering short cuts and panaceas—these can be furthered over a period of time, in a schooled people, by an education which is free of dogma, and by educators who have the courage to grapple with dangerous, because controversial, problems. More than this, schools and educators cannot legitimately do. Where they do attempt more, they become servants of the *status quo* or prophets of lost causes, more interested in salvation than in education. How much the schools can do cannot be told in advance. This always depends upon the historical situation. More specifically, it depends upon whether or not schooling in a political democracy remains (or becomes) public, universal, and free.

The historical situation today in America is one in which educators have a number of important tasks to perform. Since the conditions of effective teaching depend to a large extent upon what goes on outside the classroom, educators must vigorously oppose any measures which tend to restrict or proscribe their civic rights as members of the community. The belief that teachers are or should be political eunuchs dies hard in a society where they are selected, among other reasons, because they are "safe." At the same time they must

combat the introduction of any dogmas which would
determine the content of instruction. Some of these
dogmas are obviously political, especially where they
appear clothed as so-called "national," "racial," or
"class" truths. Some are philosophical, start from apparent truisms and end up as dangerous absurdities.
The truisms are always of a type which consists of
statements about the desirability of Order and Reason
in human affairs. As statements, they are undeniable
because either their chief terms are not defined or,
when they are, they turn out to be tautologies. The
dangerous absurdities are found in pretended deductions in which Order is now identified with a particular
kind of order, and Reason with a particular set of beliefs. The particular order and the particular beliefs
are of an era long past, acceptance of which would be
very useful to some party or church in the present.
The evidence for these beliefs is not drawn from empirical investigations, for the latter can result only in
unworthy opinion, but from the introductory truisms
about the necessity of Order and Reason in the abstract.

At the basis of both types of dogma, the political
and the philosophical, is a profound contempt for
scientific method as a method of reaching valid conclusions about human and social problems, and a subordination of scientific truths to allegedly "higher" or
"more fundamental" truths of politics and (or) theology.

The immediate bearings of Dewey's educational
theory are the same as those of his moral and social
theory. They call for a dedication to the practical

struggle for *extending* democracy by methods of intelligence in order that the methods of scientific inquiry win the authority to resolve human problems now exercised by dogma, holy or unholy, economic power, and physical force.

Chapter

X

ART AS EXPERIENCE

THE publication of John Dewey's *Art as Experience* marked, in a minor way, a turning point in the reception of his philosophy. For many years a double misinterpretation of the meaning of "instrumentalism" had stood in the way of understanding his thought. The doctrine that ideas are instruments of resolving difficulties led some to regard Dewey's whole philosophy as an apotheosis of the practical. The practical was identified with the personally useful. It was then suggested that Dewey's test of the validity of any theory in science and social affairs was the subjective utilities to be derived by acting on it.

By reading Dewey in such a way that man's chief task was to concern himself with the means and costs of practical enterprise, it was easy to charge him with neglecting to consider the ends and purposes in behalf of which all the rush and intellectual busy-work were undertaken. Like the stereotype of the American in the writings of many Europeans, he was pictured as one who continuously sacrificed the present for a future that never came, made of living a serious pursuit of the trivial, and left out of account the self-justifying experiences of love and art and understanding vision from which arise the enduring objects of allegiance of emancipated minds.

We have already seen how radically mistaken such

conceptions are. Ideas, together with correlated data
of observation, are instruments by which problematic
situations are so transformed that the original difficulties, discontinuities, and incoherences disappear. The
only sense in which thinking is invariably practical is
the sense in which it requires an operation or overt
activity at some point to reach a valid solution of the
problem. The problem may be the conventionally practical one of how to earn money or give it away; it may
be a scientific one of how to cure a disease or cause it;
it may deal with the stars, the center of the earth, or
incidents in the life of an obscure Roman who lived
thousands of years ago. The practical consequences of
knowing any particular truth must not be confused
with the practical activities by which that truth is
established. The truth *may* make us free. It *may* pros-
per us. It *may* kill us or enable us to escape being
killed.

Thinking is an experience which mediates between
other experiences. That is to say, it emerges from some
immediate experience of enjoyment or satisfaction
when some snag has been encountered; it merges into
another immediate experience after the snag has been
eliminated. Thinking, no matter what its practical
consequences, enriches the immediate experiences, the
consummations, which follow, by adding meaning to
them. In much wisdom there may be much grief, but the
experience in which wisdom ends is richer and more
significant than the bliss of ignorance. Far from sacri-
ficing immediate enjoyments and significant perceptions
of the present for *exclusively* instrumental goods,
Dewey calls attention in his ethical, social, and educational writings to the impoverishment of experience

which results from such procedure. It is one thing to assert that consummations and fulfillments cannot be stabilized without concern for means: it is another thing to assert that a life worthy of man is *merely* a continuous quest for means. Every mode of experience shows phases that are both instrumental and consummatory. But the mode of experience which we call aesthetic differs from others in that it reveals in a pre-eminent and distinctive way such an intimate coalescence of the instrumental and consummatory, that we are not conscious of any separation between them.

Although it is primarily an analysis of the roots, structure, and interrelations of the aesthetic experience, *Art as Experience* clarifies all the leading ideas of Dewey's philosophy. In addition to correcting the standard misinterpretations that have flourished among philosophers, it also constitutes the most persuasive introduction to his thought he has so far written for nonphilosophers. But it is more than this. It is that singularly rare thing—a book on aesthetics which actually enables the reader to *see* what he had not seen before, to go to objects of art and come away with a quickened apprehension of their qualities. The testimony on this point of both artists and art critics who are usually skeptical, with not a little justification, of philosophies of art, is a tribute to the sensitiveness of Dewey's insight and the faithful way in which he has let the materials and activities of the arts speak their meanings through him. Usually a philosophy of art is something that gets in the way of beholding and understanding works of art. For it is a deduction from a set of philosophical principles, not infrequently metaphysical, formulated independently of first-hand study

of subject matter, instead of a reflective summary of a
series of empirical analyses. Dewey's views on art were
not derived by asking what the experimental theory of
aesthetics must be if the philosophy of experimentalism
was to be consistent. They were shaped as a result of
direct study of the subject matter of the arts. That
they hang together with his theories of knowledge and
value gives the strength of added, because independent,
reinforcement to his several doctrines. In this chapter
we shall limit ourselves to those aesthetic themes which
show the leading principles of Dewey's philosophy at
work.

Philosophies of art have often set out as if their
function were to lay down some criterion which all
works of art must live up to in order to pass into the
gallery of imaginative creation, finally accredited by
an unmistakable tag or label. The ridiculous nature of
such an assumption is manifest in the history of art
criticism, which consists largely of a series of prohibi-
tions that artists have disregarded to the greater glory
of their art and themselves. The futility of any attempt
to find some trait which will sharply mark off, once
and for all, aesthetic objects from nonaesthetic ones is
demonstrated afresh in the clash of definitions as to
what constitutes *the* beautiful, and in controversies as
to whether the opera, the cinema, or what not *can ever*
be an art. Even at their best the conclusions reached
have such an arbitrary character that they remind
one of nothing so much as the critical theories poets
invent for the purpose of evaluating the verses of their
rivals. And when the discussion revolves around the

nature of the aesthetic experience, this is more often "explained" than described by showing that some one element—meaning or emotion or imagination—is central and everything else reducible or subordinate to it.

Dewey neither begins nor ends his inquiry with arbitrary definitions of art or of an aesthetic object. He is satisfied that any thing or activity is aesthetic "which is the object of an aesthetic experience." And aesthetic experience, like all experience, is not a private stream of consciousness but an objective interaction between a live creature and its surroundings. We should therefore expect that there are no hard and fast lines of division between aesthetic experience and other modes of experience. Rhythmic patterns of change and rest in nature and in man's body are the roots of the aesthetic experience. An aesthetic experience is present already in germ in "normal experience" wherever there is ordered doing or an appreciative perception of quality.

Not only is there a genetic continuity between aesthetic experiences and other modes of experience, practical or intellectual; it must also be recognized that the latter themselves have aesthetic quality, and that the former involve some thought or activity. What gives an experience the character it has—aesthetic, practical, or intellectual—is some *predominant* quality, not an exclusive one.

A man at work does or makes something. If he works aimlessly, or out of habit, or at command for an end assigned to him, or to meet an urgent need of action, or by mechanical rules and conventions which function like conveyor belts carrying things from somewhere to somewhere else—his experience is predominantly practical. But "the doing or making is artistic when

the perceived result is of such a nature that *its* qualities as perceived have controlled the question of production. The act of producing that is directed by intent
to produce something that is enjoyed in the immediate
experience of perceiving has qualities that a spontaneous or uncontrolled activity does not have."

A man at thought manipulates symbols that stand
for ideas or data in order to reach a conclusion. It may
then be dissociated from the process and occasion
through which he reached it, and used for other inquiries. The experience is predominantly intellectual.
But let him attend to the way in which all the steps in
the process are adapted to each other, and perceive
how they carry their cumulative meanings to a conclusion whose quality in turn discloses the significance of
the starting point of inquiry, and the experience becomes aesthetic.

On the other hand, let an artist be arrested by a
problem of getting a certain effect or discovering why
the effects already produced appear stilted or askew,
and his experience becomes intellectual. The medium of
thought is symbols but when an artist thinks—colors,
tones, images become symbols; just as, conversely,
words that are symbols of qualities in nonartistic thinking may themselves acquire intrinsic qualitative significance in a poetic experience.

In the light of these considerations Dewey is able
to show that no object is intrinsically aesthetic or nonaesthetic; that no theme or subject is inherently fit or
unfit to become the subject matter of artistic treatment; that there is no opposition (in the formal pattern of experience) between being alive in every sense
and creating or enjoying works of art; and that the

distinctions between fine and useful art are introduced by social and invidious conventions, not by intrinsic differences in the materials, techniques, or qualities of objects of art. "Any activity that is productive of objects whose perception is an immediate good, and whose operation is a constant source of enjoyable perception of other events exhibits fineness of art." Almost every other easy dualism of traditional art criticism is likewise affected by Dewey's analysis.

For all the continuities and relationships between aesthetic and nonaesthetic experiences, there is a distinctive quality of aesthetic experiences. Having shown, what has often been denied, that art is "a mode of interaction of the live creature with his environment," Dewey devotes most of his analysis to an investigation of art as a *special* mode of interaction. In what does it consist? One familiar but highly ambiguous answer is that the aesthetic experience, by which the presence of a work of art is recognized, is marked by the perception of a *qualitative unity* or *form* in any situation, object, or event.

The answer is inadequate for at least two reasons. First, qualitative unity or form is found not only where experiences are pre-eminently aesthetic but in any experience that has a distinctive character. Second, by form is sometimes meant a pattern that is abstracted from the means and material in which it is embodied, and capable like a Platonic universal of an indefinite number of incarnations. Such a conception of form can never account for the unique and intensely individualized quality of every genuine work of art. Nor can we significantly abstract some element from a work of art as its form and contrast it with other elements as

its material. Every division we make seems arbitrary
and artificial, explicable not in terms of empirical experience but of a traditional metaphysics which im-
puted an intrinsic dignity and significance to form as
a principle of rationality over against matter as the
source of imperfection. Every work of art, Dewey reminds us, is experienced as a work of *formed matter*.
Where perception recognizes the elements of a work of
art as merely conjunctive, as plot *and* character, shape
and color, objects *and* design, sound *and* meaning,
structure *and* function, etc., we are in the presence of a
defective work of art. *Aesthetic* form is present to the
extent that these elements are so organized in relation
to each other that they evoke a direct and vital perceptual experience of unique integration.

This direct and unified perception is not instanta-
neous. We may feel at a glance, but the feeling is not
yet an aesthetic perception. At most, this feeling is an
experience of what Dewey calls "a seizure," in which
something catches or strikes us, we know not why or
how, except that it registers in visceral effects. This
seizure is an organic reaction to an undifferentiated
totality out of which an aesthetic perception *may* develop. It is as often a form of bewilderment as of rap-
ture. It has no authentic aesthetic status until certain
conditions are fulfilled in subsequent phases of experience. These conditions can only be stated in general
form, for, as we go from art to art, differences in
media and means will somewhat affect their order and
formulation. Dewey lists them as cumulation, tension
or opposition, conservation, anticipation or suspense,
and fulfillment.

(a) Before the actual and complete aesthetic perception takes place, irrespective of whether it be a play, a novel, a painting, a piece of music, there is a cumulation of sensory effects and meanings, "a progressive massing of values," which indicates that the details of action or scene cohere with each other, and that they are building up or leading to something. (b) At some point in the process of cumulation, a tension or resistance is aroused by the suggestion of contrasting or opposing patterns of coherence. It is marked by a questioning. What is going on? Is the lead this way or that? Why this arresting detail or act or word—here and now? "Without internal tension there would be a fluid rush to a straightaway mark: there would be nothing that could be called development and fulfillment." The points of tension and resistance are the focal points of understanding in art. For they create the difficulties. Subsequent perception must be of such a character that the initial obstacles, ambiguities, and dissonances are grasped as the intended means of achieving certain effects. (c) Conservation and modification of the original suggested pattern of development, as well as of the tensions of conflicting possible eventuations, are necessary if more and more of the elements disclosed to eye or ear are to be assimilated. The work of art cannot stop short with a question, a riddle, or a doubt unless that is its intended culmination, in which case it has not stopped short but come to an appropriate close. (d) The discovery of aesthetic form requires an anticipation of how the development of line, action, or musical phrase will be completed. Knowledge that there is some ready-made antecedent scheme toward which things in some way or other must move detracts from the excellence of the work of art.

That which is about to be must have an adequate preparation in what has been; but it must not overdetermine what is to follow, otherwise there is no element of novelty or unexpectedness and the conclusion appears obvious or banal. (e) The fulfillment or realization of the anticipation is the most heightened phase of the aesthetic experience. Perception is richer because it takes up into itself all of the strands that have been previously observed and fuses them into an intense, unified, and significant experience. Anticipation and fulfillment in the production or perception of a work of art is not a final and all-embracing synthesis. There is a whole series of anticipations and fulfillments as observation unfolds. Each close is experienced as dramatically appropriate and carries over to the next pulse of perception as well as to subsequent occasions when the work of art is viewed afresh. "There is no final term in the appreciation of a work of art. It carries on and is, therefore, instrumental as well as final."

There are two things that must be borne in mind if Dewey's account is not to be shrugged aside as another unverifiable "psychology" of art, where "psychology" refers to purely mental processes. The first is that whether or not the object of art meets the conditions enumerated above is to be determined by an *empirical* observation of what is found in it, not by reports of introspective experience. Whether a character is consistently drawn; whether conflict, opposition, and tension exist—all of these things can be established by studying how the work of art organizes the "means and materials that belong to the common and public world." The artist begins with a personal vision. But he expresses it to himself and others by what he does

—in observable effects. Every quality is the result of some property of technique, arrangement, medium, whose presence or absence is in principle as testable and verifiable as any other entity in the physical world. The possession of aesthetic form is objectively determinable just as soon as specific meaning has been given to the general conditions which an object must meet in order to become an object of art.

The second consideration is that the discoverable properties of a work of art do not inhere in its "physical materials and energies" independently of the directed activity and energies of the live creature. The qualities of a work of art are not just out there in the physical materials even when the latter are selectively arranged. The human being must do something in relation to them, he must take them in a certain way, before what is distinctively aesthetic is apprehended. To attribute aesthetic quality is tantamount to saying to someone: "Do such and such, and you will perceive this and that." What is perceived is not *in* the object; nor *in* the subject; but in the interacting relation of the two.

The human contribution to aesthetic experience is not only biological but social. An individual looks at a work of art through the eyes of a whole tradition. Let a marked shift in historical and social perspective take place and a work of art may become just another thing—peculiar or commonplace. Even when all the physical materials and energies of a work of art remain unaltered, it has a history as an art object. The variations in its history can be significantly correlated with changes in the climate of opinion. There is no permanent aesthetic form waiting to be discovered like a river or mountain or treasure buried in the ground. Something is lost when the funded meanings of the period in which the work of art was produced become obsolescent; something is gained when it is introduced into another cultural milieu and operates to intensify and deepen the qualities of experience. Aesthetic form is reformed because of what the acculturated organism brings to the occasions of experience.

If the general conditions which a work must fulfill to acquire aesthetic status are accepted, the function of criticism is therewith indicated. It is simply "an act of intelligence performed upon the matter of direct perception in the interest of a more adequate perception." The measure of its value is its success in sending us back to the object of art to see what we had not seen before. It enables our perceptual experience to move more easily to fulfillment. By discriminating judgments it makes accessible to us the objective relationships between the constituent elements of the aesthetic whole which had previously been obscure because of a new idiom or technique or our own lack of sensibility. Such a conception of criticism presents the only alternative that can steer clear of the dogmatism of "judicial" criticism and the irresponsibility of "impressionism."

Judicial criticism is usually an appendage of the art style which "has arrived." It makes the possession of aesthetic form as such synonymous with the exhibition of some familiar technique. The significance of the fact that the latter has had a history is ignored. Like its counterparts in education and morals, such criticism

identifies order and balance with a particular kind of
ordering and balancing. Departures from it which express new modes of interaction between man and the
world are regarded with suspicion. They are frequently
ruled out by definitions that are really descriptions of
yesterday's creative achievement. The persistent attempt of trying to say what is new is characterized
as a cult of the unintelligible.

Impressionist criticism is born out of a justified re-
vulsion to the smugness and cramping influence of
judicial criticism. But it is criticism only by courtesy.
By telling us what the work of art means to him, how
it affects him, what it reminds him of, the critic is
calling attention away from the work of art itself. At
its best such criticism results in the production of another work of art, what is sometimes called "creative
criticism." Where this is not the case, no principle of
relevance unifies the whimsical or passionate or anec-
dotal outpourings of impressionist criticism. Insofar
as it defends its emancipation from control by the object of art, it falls back upon a sweeping denial of any
kind of objective values in art. It asserts truly that the
actual impression or judgment of a work of art—no
matter whose, artist's or perceiver's—occurs "at a
given moment." It infers falsely that the import and
validity of an impression at a given moment are themselves "affairs of a passing moment." Insofar as it acts
on this false inference, it runs out into an excited
volubility.

Since criticism is judgment, it is better or worse depending upon the insight, knowledge, and evidence that
can be marshaled in its support. The more concerned

judgment is with the relevant details of craftsmanship,
related meanings, and the qualities of the medium in
interpreting a work of art, the more effective it is in
enriching our perception of the value of the work as a
whole. Judgment which tries to state in one summary
phrase the worth of a work of art as a whole is not
very illuminating. It results in terms like "grand,"
"beautiful," "ugly," which are more often exclamations
of emotion than sensitive perceptions of objective qualities. The critics' statements, insofar as they are relevant, true or false, should be directed to those aspects
of the work of art which show how its matter has been
formed. The object of the critic's analysis is therefore,
strictly speaking, something which is always short of
the whole. The effect of his judgments may lead us to
have a new experience of the work of art as a whole,
but the content of his judgments are the specific relationships which its parts bear to each other. His task
does not culminate in a flat pronouncement but in an
invitation to have *an* experience. In brief, to be critical
is to make judgments. To make judgments is to claim
to have knowledge, not merely general knowledge about
classes of works of art but knowledge about this particular work of art. To perceive with knowledge is to
perceive more richly and intensely.

The knowledge necessary for intelligent criticism
must be relevant, i.e., it must understand what are
sometimes called the immanent qualities and relations
in a work of art. The qualities and relations that are
in the work of art may sometimes take us out of the
work of art to social, economic, and religious conditions
and causes. But when we begin with the latter as gen-

eral conditions and causes of the art of a period, and then interpret individual works of art as "expressions" of the *Zeitgeist,* or mode of economic production, or what not, we are in the cloudy skies of mystical sociology. The same causes or social milieu may be "expressed" in objects of art of the most varied aesthetic quality, just as they may be expressed in statements about nature which range from true to false to meaningless. The primary concern of the art critic is precisely with those differences in immanent quality which makes for a full and complete aesthetic experience in one case, and a stunted or arrested experience in another; just as the task of scientific criticism of statements about nature is to distinguish between the meaningless and meaningful, the probably true and the probably false.

To be sure, aesthetic experience, as Dewey himself points out, "is always more than aesthetic." It signifies something about nature, about society, about the specific culture in which it occurs. We may legitimately ask: What effect does the aesthetic experience have on other modes of experience? What is the role of art in civilization? We do not have to be artists or critics to ask such questions. For they are themes in the philosophy of civilization and culture, important themes because our morals, our education, our social programs are in part shaped by the answers we give.

One of the most impressive functions of art in civilization is one that is least intended, namely, its role in establishing the continuity of culture. More than any

other one thing, it is the arts of previous cultures—
their architecture, sculpture, ornament, literature—
which give us a sense of the presence of the past in the
present. It is to the arts that we turn to find the keys
of understanding to the pervasive qualities of the civilization of which they were a part, and to its characteristic modes of experience.

Why should art be so pre-eminently eloquent about
the meanings of a culture, more so than roads, methods
of work or war, and even religions? Because it is a
mode of communal life whose subject and subject matters are furnished by all other modes of life. The
aesthetic strain in human experience is woven out of
qualities found in everyday affairs but rendered more
intense in virtue of direct perception. In our own society, but much more in previous societies, "art is the
extension of the power of rites and ceremonies to unite
men, through a shared celebration, to all incidents and
scenes of life." When we speak of the style, the pattern,
the form, the collective individuality of a culture, our
very language testifies to the fact that it is to the arts
that we look for the qualitative unity which marks off
one culture from other cultures. For art expresses the
most deep-seated and generic attitudes in an epoch,
that which defines the congenial and uncongenial, the
native and foreign, what is within the range of imagination and what not.

It is natural, therefore, that Dewey should urge the
cultivation of the arts in our own culture as an effective agency of facilitating communication between
different peoples and groups. By enlarging our sympathies and horizons of vision, art deepens understand-

ing. Differences in tastes, manners, and morals could not be evaluated in a spirit of fierce parochialism, were the objects in which these differences are expressed occasions for wide and genuine aesthetic perception. It is not only cultural differences which are bridged by artistic experience. The isolations, gaps, and barriers between individuals melt away in the warmth of common enjoyments. Participation in a common art tends to make subsequent communication freer and easier. Art is the truly universal mode of language between individuals as well as nations. "The differences between English, French, and German speech create barriers that are submerged when art speaks."

The role that art can play in present-day culture is far from the one it does play. The same set of institutions which obstruct the use of intelligence limit the opportunities for the emergence of sustaining aesthetic qualities in ordinary living. Art has too much of a museum character. Industry that produces for profit cannot concern itself with the aesthetic effects of commodities except insofar as they pay. It reinforces as a consequence the invidious distinctions between the fine and useful arts. The uncertain conditions of employment and the absence of self-government in industrial life prevent millions of workers from acquiring that type of interest in what they do which is essential to aesthetic satisfaction. There is little consciousness of the significance of useful work, even when it is well done.

All this could be changed in a planning society in which intelligence would organize social resources with a never-failing eye for the aesthetic strain in production and consumption. What sensitive people do today in furnishing a room in order to enjoy a restful perception, society could do on a large scale in relation to our housing, our machine products—whether it be clothes, instruments, or furniture—our roadsides, our cities, down to the very quarters which abut on railroad tracks. Even from the standpoint of art, a sufficient basis exists for profound changes in our social relationships. "Art itself is not secure under modern conditions until the mass of men and women who do the useful work of the world have the opportunity to be free in conducting the processes of production, and are richly endowed in capacity for enjoying the fruits of collective work."

As we have seen, a planning society can achieve these promises of free experience in a hungerless world, only insofar as its practices, as well as its faith, are both democratic and scientific. Their absence in such a society would spell the most horrible form of tyranny to which human beings have ever been subjected. Most horrible because fortified by all the refinements of modern technology and propaganda. Our willingness to adopt and defend the democratic and scientific way of life ultimately depends upon our belief in their capacity to improve the quality of human experience. The belief is self-critical without being viciously circular. But it can be made more significant by becoming subject and subject matter of art. It is possible for art to remain free and still find sources of inspiration in the adventure of the scientific quest and the richness of communal experience. Science seems to be foreign to the interests of modern art, and democracy is only a

political catchword to most artists. Dewey's hope is
that some day they may bear the same relation—but
uncoerced—to the art of our time that religion and
nationalism have borne to the arts of previous cultures.

Chapter

XI

NATURE AND MAN

RELIGIONS and religious philosophies find something lacking in the philosophy of John Dewey. Some call it religion. Some call it metaphysics. But all sense the absence of concern with questions about what are sometimes called "the ultimate mysteries of existence." Why does the world exist, and what is its origin? Where do we come from and where are we going? What can a man believe and what can a man hope about human destiny? Some see in such queries an expression of "metaphysical hunger" that cannot be stilled by the knowledge of all the sciences in and of the world.

It would indeed be surprising if those who are absorbed in such themes did not find something lacking in Dewey's philosophy. For instead of the attempt to find a first cause or a final goal in existence, Dewey offers us an analysis of why all such questions make assumptions that render them self-defeating. They are self-defeating because in principle no observation or logical inferences drawn from observations can ever verify a statement whose subject is *the* whole universe, *the* totality, *the* scheme of things entire. Genuine problems and questions are always specific. They are always such that we can tell what would constitute evidence one way or another to make the answers to them more or less probable.

When we do appear to speak meaningfully about the

world or the universe, it is by way of an ellipsis. We may sometimes say of an individual that "He accepts or denies the universe," but such expressions refer to his observable attitudes in a series of experiences. By enlarging the series of experiences to include those yet to come, we get a conception of the universe which Dewey calls "an imaginative totality." We can never reach the all inclusive totality of existences and possibilities which many metaphysicians have regarded as the subject of judgments that are true or false. Or we may say "The world is problematic," but this is only shorthand for "Men face problems of determinate kinds —social, personal, political, technological, etc." To specific questions, only specific investigations of the specific conditions and changes which constitute the situation under inquiry can be relevant. As Dewey puts it, "Once admit that the sole verifiable or fruitful object of knowledge is the particular set of changes that generate the object of study together with the consequences that then flow from it, and no intelligible question can be asked about what, by assumption, lies outside."

Whoever then looks to Dewey to find out whether God or chance is the cause of the universe, whether the soul of man is immortal, whether life is good, bad, or has an absolute meaning, is doomed to disappointment.

Yet, although Dewey has no answer to these questions, he understands why they are asked. They express human bewilderment, fear, perplexity, and curiosity in a world whose vast forces make living a perilous career. Even at its best, human control is uncertain. Our planet is bathed in cosmic energies which may some day render it uninhabitable. The sources from which human beings replenish their vital energies are unknown to us. We may breed idiocy out of the human race, but who will guarantee the sanity of the breeder? Poverty and justice are always relative; and inequalities a constant source not only of desirable variety but of hate and strife. It is doubtful whether there will ever be a planned society that will provide "the sumptuosity of security" for which so many leave this world of ordinary experience to dwell in rapt visions of a hereafter. No one who takes distance to the specific problems of experience can escape taking an attitude to the conditions out of which they arise. For even when we have seen through the pretensions of metaphysics and religion "to explain things," even when we have turned completely and wholeheartedly to science to solve whatever problems can be solved, there still remain the conditions of common experience toward which we must define an attitude—call it emotional, religious, personal. "When man, individually and collectively, has done his uttermost, conditions that at different times and places have given rise to the ideas of Fate and Fortune, of Chance and Providence, remain."

Nothing is easier than to attribute a benevolent or malevolent intent to natural forces in relation to human aspiration. Traditional religion personifies benevolence into a directing agency and wrestles with the difficulties its own faith creates. Traditional atheism often takes on a theological character by viewing human destiny as the unrolling of preordained doom in an unequal battle against the blind powers of nature.

Dewey believes that it is possible to have a sense of dependence upon, and humility before, the cosmic forces on which we must rely even when we build shelters

against them, without surrendering to supernaturalism
or to the simple negativism of village atheism. Supernaturalism as a creed is hard to accept for a person
of intelligence and courage; atheism as a doctrine iso-
lates man from those relations of the physical world
which support human achievement. Natural piety recognizes the continuity between man and nature. It ac-
knowledges man's kinship of origin, but not of interest
or aim, with other living things. It accepts the natural
limitation imposed upon man's effort by the fact that
he has a body, that he is a creature of time, history,
and society, as a point of departure for improving the
human estate. In this way natural piety avoids the
servility of those who fear the gods and would placate
them, as well as the arrogance of those who would be
gods. "Natural piety is not of necessity either a fatal-
istic acquiescence in natural happenings or a romantic
idealization of the world. It may rest upon a just sense
of nature as the whole of which we are parts, while it
also recognizes that we are parts that are marked by
intelligence and purpose, having the capacity to strive
by their aid to bring conditions into greater consonance with what is humanly desirable. Such piety is
an inherent constituent of a just perspective in life."

Words such as these lend themselves to easy misinterpretation especially if their poetic form is read with
a syntactic literalness. Dewey speaks of "nature as the
whole of which we are parts." To some this may suggest an organic relation of part and whole such that
did man not exist nature would not; or such that the
existence of nature necessitates the existence of man.
This is a doctrine very close to Hegel's objective idealism, according to which all things are necessarily in-

terrelated, where "necessarily interrelated" means
"logically interrelated." And since Dewey was a Hegelian
in his early years and never hesitated to acknowledge
that he learned from Hegel, he has been charged with
"holism," "organicism," "teleological idealism," all variant terms for the doctrine that there is some logical
or moral reason in the nature of things why man must
appear when and where he does. In other words, because Dewey stresses continuities, even among things
that are sharply opposed to each other, the belief in an
all-embracing, meaningful continuity is attributed to
him. That at the same time other critics should complain of his stress upon the irreducible pluralities of
experience indicates that we are here confronted with
another radical misconception of the philosophy of experimentalism.

In Dewey's opinion, the term continuity is correla-
tive with the term discontinuity. Consequently, to say
that all things in the world are continuous with each
other is not to say anything significant until the specific respect is indicated in which the continuity
consists. The assertion of the existence of any specific
continuity must be empirically established. The continuity of the earth, the sun, and stars is established by
physics and astronomy; of man's body with nature by
biology; of his mind and body by psychology; of his
personality and the personality of others by sociology
and education. The continuities may be genetic, spatial,
cultural. And so may be the discontinuities. Both are
found in experience. When Dewey speaks then of man
as a part of the whole of nature, he is making a synop-
tic reference to the multitudes of connections, correlations, and dependences which the sciences have shown

to exist between men, societies, and the physical world. The significance of the statement has no moral import except when taken in conjunction with the qualification that man is a part of nature "marked by intelligence and purpose" by whose aid he strives to build a more desirable world. We can strive to build a more desirable world only when the world in which we already live is experienced as deficient, incomplete, uncertain. These traits are as objective as any others. They mark the points of discontinuity within our experience—the centers of trouble and peril. Intelligence consists in acting with and upon the specific continuities that run through given situations in order to eliminate their specific discontinuities.

For Hegel, there is in the last analysis only one situation—the Totality, the Absolute, God, of which other situations are partial phases. For Dewey, first and last, there are any number of situations, some sharply marked off from each other, some shading into each other, some of them relevant and most of them irrelevant to one another. For Hegel, the precarious character of our experience is an illusion bred of a finite point of view. Philosophical progress consists in seeing that "the real" is ideal and that the ideal is already "real." For Dewey, the contingent and precarious nature of existence is no more illusory than any of the qualities into which metaphysics would sublimate them. "We live in a world which is an impressive and irresistible mixture of sufficiencies, tight completenesses, order, recurrences which make possible prediction and control, and singularities, ambiguities, uncertain possibilities, processes going on to consequences as yet indeterminate."

Dewey's theory of experience throws additional light on what he conceives man's place in nature to be. He admits freely, gladly, and with a frequency which should confound all who insist upon finding a pew for him in the church of Bishop Berkeley, that existence and experience are not synonymous. Experience is a special kind of existence. It is found only where creatures of comparatively highly organized nervous systems are alive. To be alive is to interact with and in the particular environment which supports life. Experience, then, is not something which occurs in the mind when man meets nature and through which he looks as if it were a screen, diaphanous or translucent, upon a world outside of himself. To be human is already to be interacting, is to be having experiences.

These experiences indicate what nature is here and now. They also enable us to tell what nature was or will be there and then. Our starting point is this special kind of existence which we call experience. Through inquiry we can discover something about existences which are not experiences. Whether it is a genuine discovery or a conceit depends upon *what* is experienced and *how*, here and now. Between the experience we start with and the experience with which we end, there intervenes the process of finding out. Finding out is an experience. In its controlled and systematic form it is the activity which we call science. Like all experiences, it is a mode of interaction between man and his environment. In this interaction some physical changes are set up in the situation under investigation. The results of the process of finding out are scientific objects and laws. It is at this point that a tragic mistake is made. The scientific objects and laws, existences to which we

are led by the experience of finding out, are called
"nature," "reality," "what things actually are in their
own right," and contrasted with experience which now
becomes "appearance," "subjective states of mind,"
"immediate data." A qualityless nature and an object-
less experience result. Nature and experience are set
over against one another as alien and opposed existences. "We get the absurdity of an experiencing which
experiences only itself, states and processes of consciousness, instead of the things of nature." From this
a few short steps lead to all the dualisms which we have
previously discussed, and few more steps to a theoretical subjectivism which because it cannot be seriously
acted upon has been well called "silly."

For Dewey, nature is not something which is merely
known but something which is acted upon, used, and
enjoyed. Whatever traits are revealed in the various
modes of experience are equally natural, but not all of
them are equally reliable for the special purposes of
knowing or playing or fighting. Nothing is given in
experience which is not also taken; nothing is under-
gone which is not also acted upon. Man's life is a serial
process of interacting energies in which nature is a
co-operating and supporting factor. Only men have intent, but, without natural mechanisms and structure,
human intent would be what Santayana calls consciousness, nothing but "a lyric cry." Once cut the cords of
connection which bind man to nature even when he
strives to improve on it, and there is no escape from
the agonizing view, in all its variants from the Book
of Ecclesiastes to the Notebooks of Kierkegaard, that
"the self [is] not merely a pilgrim but an unnaturalized
and unnaturalizable alien in this world."

In defining his attitude Dewey distinguishes it sharply from that of religion with its dogmas, creeds, and institutional appurtenances. If man must find a consolation for the imperfections of experience, it should be based on knowledge not on myth. If he needs ideals to make a unity rather than a miscellany out of his experiences, he must search them out from among his own possibilities of integration rather than accept a revelation from some spokesmen of the supernatural that they are already embodied in existence. There is a great difference according to Dewey between having a religion and being religious. To have a religion is to be committed to a set of doctrines about this world, and usually about a next, which cannot be scientifically validated and at some point runs counter to scientific evidence. To be religious is to give unqualified allegiance to an imaginative ideal, based on the heart's deepest desire, which directs our fundamental choices, and does not yield before the tyranny of force and chance. It is not knowledge, although based on knowledge. A man may be religious about science, art, his country, or aiding people in distress. It is a quality revealed whenever we stake our life on a pledge, a cause, a commitment. We are religious about the things that we would rather die than do or leave undone. Religious faith, says Dewey, is "the unification of the self through allegiance to inclusive ideal ends which imagination presents to us and to which the human will responds as worthy of controlling our desires and choices." The God of religious faith, understood in this sense, is not a Person, a Power, or even an embodied Ideal. It is simply another name for "the unity of all ideal ends arousing us to desire and actions."

Although there may be fewer people who are religious than have religions, on Dewey's own view it follows that there is even more diversification among the former than among the latter. There are many gods because there are many inclusive ideal ends. What is Dewey religious about? What is his God? It is not hard to guess. If there are any absolutes in his outlook, they are intelligence and democracy, or the ideal of a scientific, democratic community. They are absolute because as inclusive values they are also inclusive methods which enable us to test existing values and create others. It is unlikely that they can ever be completely rooted out, even in a robot state; but even if they were, they would still deserve to live, they would still be worthy of human allegiance and struggle.

The religious attitude, according to Dewey, takes us out of the narrow circles of personal concern. Without it, professions of justice to all are hollow, and respect for the dignity of human beings, a phrase. It ties us in imagination with the generations that have preceded and those that will follow. It is not a worship of nature or humanity in the large, for a natural force is something to control, not to bow down to, and men are often cruel and ignorant. It is a faith that makes us sensitive to the common needs of our common lot and gives us the courage to strive continuously not only for our own betterment but for that of our fellowmen. Whatever spirituality traditional religion has had flows from the religious faith that we are all members of one another's body, which, sincerely acted upon, would lead to the end of all religious division. But no one can describe Dewey's religious faith—one that he offers as "a common faith"—better than he himself. "The things

in civilization we most value are not of ourselves. They
exist by the grace of the continuous human community
in which we are a link. Ours is the responsibility of
conserving, transmitting, rectifying and expanding the
heritage of values we have received that those who
come after us may receive it more solid and secure,
more widely accessible and more generously shared
than we have received it. Here are all the elements for a
religious faith that shall not be confined to sect, class
or race."

Why does Dewey use the term "God" for the imaginative projection of a set of ideal goals as a directing
force in human experience? He justifies his use on the
grounds that he needs a distinctive word, and that there
is some historic usage which warrants its employment
in this sense. Not a few thinkers in the history of culture who rejected the content of traditional supernaturalism have nonetheless used its language: Spinoza,
Shelley, Paine, Feuerbach. As usual, however, some
theologians have seized upon the term in Dewey's writings to read into it their own conception of the supernatural. Despite the fact that they have been sharply
reprimanded by Dewey, it is safe to predict that others
will continue the practice. Many who remain within
the organized churches will react to Dewey's reference
to "God" and "the divine" in human experience somewhat like Gretchen to Faust's explanation of where he
stood on religion. There are so many misconceptions of
Dewey's philosophy it seems a pity that his language
at this point should invite more.

Looking away from the verbal peculiarities in which
Dewey's cosmic outlook is expressed, we cannot fail to
note how it recaptures the impressive quality of classic

serenity at the same time as it retains the modern feeling for activity. Peace of mind may be easily purchased by withdrawal and resignation. It may also be found, but without tincture of fear, in intelligent action. Dewey's view contains something of the grandeur of the Stoic tradition without its emotional impoverishment, and without its confusion of physics and ethics. It is anthropocentric in the sense that it recognizes that man brings something of himself to his every experience, and leaves the world a different place for his having been there. It is naturalistic because it recognizes that human experience is itself natural, that its existence is no more and no less miraculous than anything else, and that it can learn to be at home in the only world it will ever know. Creature of nature as man is, he can live and die as a human being. The life of man is not an aspiration to divinity, but a courageous struggle to uphold ideals which the universe makes possible but which he alone can make actual. Dewey's credo shines through everything he writes, but it appears clearest in the memorable passages of *Experience and Nature*, from which the following lines are taken.

"When we have used our thought to its utmost and have thrown into the moving unbalanced balance of things our puny strength, we know that though the universe slay us still we may trust, for our lot is one with whatever is good in existence. We know that such thought and effort is one condition of the coming into existence of the better. As far as we are concerned it is the only condition, for it alone is in our power. To ask more than this is childish; but to ask less is a recreance no less egotistic, involving no less a cutting of ourselves from the universe than does the expectation that it meet and satisfy our every wish. To ask in good faith as much as this from ourselves is to stir into motion every capacity of imagination, and to exact from action every skill and bravery."

An account of Dewey's faith would be incomplete which did not communicate the place of *creative* intelligence within it. We have already seen how his theory of experience as well as his theory of logic stresses the interactive and reconstructive phases of all human behavior. When we take them in conjunction with what Dewey says about the "working union of the ideal with the actual," it becomes clear that "acceptance" of the world is a condition for effective activity. Such acceptance is not synonymous with acquiescence or prostrate resignation, for some portion of the world, however small, is different as a consequence of it.

The interactions of exclusively physical processes, even where patterns are repeated, generate a stream of novel qualities. When human beings enter into interaction, because of the complex character of the nervous system and the existence of social relationships charged with meaning, the range of variations in qualities is increased. Problems of adjustment and control become momentous since choices can be made that will shut out or open up certain kinds of interaction. Human intelligence is an instrument for creating or modifying the conditions by which the variation of qualities may be extended or restricted in line with our choice.

To extend the range of novel experience costs trouble and involves risk. It is not surprising that there are many who feel that their existence is sufficiently prob-

lematic without thirsting for novel experiences and
adventures. When this attitude becomes deep-seated, intelligence is used to institute safe and sane routines.
The tried, the familiar, the established in thought and
practice are, wherever possible, given preference. Preference develops into habit and habit into second nature.
A feeling of distrust and vague apprehension is built
up toward variety and novelty which can always justify
itself because it is precisely under these forms that
shocks and disappointments appear. There are many
lives in which the maxim, "No news is good news, and
the less news the better," serves not only in times of
crisis but in organizing all avenues of experience.

Dewey's attitude is one which welcomes variety as a
positive value. Not a variety of evils, of course, but a
variety of significant experiences. He prefers that virtues be thick and rich and even a little mixed rather
than thin, ascetic, and correctly dull. The function of
intelligence is—perhaps it would be better to say,
could be—not merely to make existing goods secure,
not merely to fend off the unwanted, but to increase
the possibility of fresh and novel activity. It conserves
and harmonizes existing values but also liberates new
values. One of the reasons why his own ideals are wedded so firmly to the democratic way of life is that its
patterns make possible, where intelligence is at work,
a richness of co-operating diversities that contrasts
sharply with the fixed patterns stamped on the minds,
even on the bodies, of individuals in regimented societies.

Where things change in time, novelties result from all
experiences. Where things change as a consequence
of applied intelligence, novelties have moral and cul-

tural import. In remaking parts of the world, we re-
make ourselves. The generic form of all responsibility
is being responsive to possibilities of change. The power
of intelligence is limited. Nonetheless, once directed to
the multiplication of the material and ideal goods of
living, to the shaping of occasions for joyous and
shared experience, it is powerful enough to transform
the existing social order down to its very bedrock and
to create a society of freedom and fellowship.

This, too, is part of John Dewey's faith.

Chapter

XII

THE PHILOSOPHER OF AMERICAN DEMOCRACY

A LEADING principle in Dewey's interpretations of the thought of other philosophers is that every influential philosophy reflects, by way of criticism or justification, some features of the social life of its times. Turn about is fair play as well as necessary in the interests of intellectual consistency. It is legitimate to inquire into the features of our own time and society which are reflected in John Dewey's philosophy. Since his origins, his training, his sphere of activity and influence have been essentially American, we may narrow the scope of our question to the American scene.

Critics have not been slow to put Dewey under the same social fluoroscope through which he has examined the vital motivations of his predecessors. Even philosophers who have proclaimed that sociological analyses of philosophy are not worth the paper they are written on have discoursed at length on the relation between Dewey's ideas and American life. The results of these inquiries have often proved more illuminating about the critic's fear or dislike of American culture than in disclosing significant connections between the philosophy of experimentalism and the saga of American life. Perhaps this is due to the fact that all such inquiry must perform a double task of interpretation—of

American culture as well as of Dewey's ideas. And neither is easy.

One facile literary critic has seen in Dewey's philosophy little but a continuation of "the pragmatic acquiescence" to the dreary compromises, the externalism, and cruelties of American life which had received an earlier expression in the philosophy of William James. (A single reading of James's letters is sufficient to reveal the emptiness of the charge against the man who wrote that "callousness to abstract justice is *the* sinister feature of United States civilization.") The chief reason, apparently, for this blanket judgment on Dewey, aside from a misreading of a text, is his failure to oppose America's entry into the World War to save democracy. By a strange irony, this very critic, at the present writing, is frantically beating the tom-toms for another world war for peace and democracy. Stranger still, in a retrospective evaluation, he justifies America's entry into the last war, so that, in to his latest pronouncements, Dewey should be applauded for having acquiesced in the acquiescence of the American people.

Today Dewey is one of the nation's leaders in the antiwar movement. As for his stand in 1917, only those of Dewey's critics who themselves followed Eugene V. Debs can afford to cast any stones. It is true that he did not actively oppose the War. His knowledge of the economics and politics of imperialism was inadequate, and he placed too much confidence in Woodrow Wilson's new deal in foreign policy. He has admitted that the experience was highly instructive. But it is also true that he spent more energy defending the civil liberties that were sacrificed during the War than in aiding its prosecution. He indicated the reasons for his half-heartedness in a striking essay, "In a Time of National Hesitation," published while America was at war. Speaking of the conditions under which hesitation could be replaced by whole-heartedness, he wrote: "Not until the almost impossible happens, not until the Allies are fighting on our terms for our democracy and civilization, will that happen." In subsequent essays he made clear that by "our democracy and civilization" he meant not the entirety of existing practices in American life but those aspects which were in consonance with, or could be brought in consonance with, the ideals of freedom, and equality of opportunity for individual development.

The main point of this discussion of Dewey's attitude to the War, which really belongs in his biography rather than in this study, is to show how absurd it is to isolate his stand on *one* political event as evidence of the "real" cultural significance of his philosophy.

The most popular type of sociological analysis of Dewey's thought was evolved by European critics when they were first confronted by the philosophical monster born across the seas. It was then taken over by spokesmen of the genteel tradition in America and still flourishes in variant forms wherever we are invited to take our troubles to eternity instead of trying to settle them here and now. This type of analysis is exemplified in many of the remarks made about pragmatism by Bertrand Russell during his period as a Platonic realist. Although since that time he has on occasions called pragmatism the philosophic expression of the logic of scientific method, he still lapses into the social criticism of earlier days. The following is a characteristic judgment: "I find love of truth in America obscured by commercialism of which pragmatism is the philosophical expression; and love of our neighbor kept in fetters by Puritan morality." In other quarters, and sometimes by Russell himself, pragmatism, because of its alleged hostility to art, useless play, and the joys of sheer animal exuberance, is linked with Puritanism.

This judgment on American culture does not concern us here although it does seem curious that anyone in the face of recent European history should intimate the superior virtue of European precept and practice in respect to truth and love of neighbor. Least of all Bertrand Russell, who has been imprisoned because of his love for truth and persecuted because of his love for his neighbor. The judgment which identifies pragmatism as the philosophical expression of commercialism does concern us. For despite its currency, it is unscientific and superficial. It can sincerely be held only by those who understand pragmatism to mean that the truth of an idea depends upon the amount of money one can make by believing it, or by getting others to believe it; which would make every successful confidence man a pragmatist instead of a candidate for a post in some European Foreign Office. There is no way of meeting a criticism of this sort except by inviting those who make it to give reasons for their statement, and, if they point to James's metaphor about "the cash-value" of ideas, inviting them to learn the American language. The same method of interpretation applied to the critics' own philosophy would make them wild if it were taken as anything but a witticism. For, as Dewey in a delicious passage points out with specific reference to Russell, to regard pragmatism as the inlectual expression of commercialism "is of that order of

interpretation which would say that English neo-real-
ism is a reflection of the aristocratic snobbery of the
English; the tendency of French thought to dualism
an expression of an alleged Gallic disposition to keep
a mistress in addition to a wife; and the idealism of
Germany a manifestation of an ability to elevate beer
and sausage into a higher synthesis with the spiritual
values of Beethoven and Wagner."

Some of the criticisms emanating from those who believe that all philosophy is economically determined
have been no less grotesque. According to one critic,
the philosophy of Dewey is an apologia for American
finance capitalism. Another of the same doctrinal persuasion tones this down to make Dewey the spokesman
of the reactionary petty bourgeoisie, which dislikes
trustified capitalism but hates socialism even more. A
third hears in him the voice of Populist America, presumably singing experimental tenor to Bryan's funda-
mentalist bass.

A minor apologist of Russian totalitarianism finds in
good dialectic fashion that Dewey's philosophy reflects
both "the expanding phase of capitalism" and "its decline." How it reflects the expanding phase of capitalism we are not clearly told but it reflects the decline
because Dewey's *Individualism—Old and New*, "his depression book," published in 1930, marked his break
with capitalism and acceptance of socialism. "Oppressed
with the increasing dislocation and misery of our economic order, Dewey cast about for a solution." Unfortunately for the critic, all of the leading ideas of the
book, including the major portions of the manuscript,
had been written and some even published, before the
crisis of 1929, at a time when belief in the myth of un-

ending prosperity was quite general. And so what is really a tribute to Dewey's foresight, sensitiveness, and courage is used as evidence that his scientific philosophy is sadly inferior to the dialectical logic of the Communist Party line. But the joke is on the critic, for the convolutions of that party line have followed so closely the erratic course, laid down by its pilots in the Kremlin, that it is now at positions which Dewey abandoned as mistaken years ago.

The record of types of social misinterpretations of John Dewey's philosophy would not be complete without reference to the view promulgated in many Catholic centers of higher learning that in Dewey's thought all the insidious and un-American tendencies of our national life come to expression. This is done by coolly identifying Americanism with the scholastic philosophy, and denouncing as a dangerous heresy practically all of modern philosophy. I quote a representative statement which requires no further comment. "The fundamental law of the United States and the institutions that have been raised upon that Constitution are grounded in scholastic philosophy—the philosophy of Aristotle, Aquinas, and Edmund Burke. . . . The professor who teaches American youth the false philosophies of Hegel and Kant and Croce and Dewey as ideals—that professor is a thousand times more a dictatorial or communist threat than if he wore a brown shirt and steel helmet or waved the murderous red flag of the Soviet."

Dewey is an American philosopher, and many features of American life and tradition do find expression

in his philosophy. One does not have to go fishing in
the muddy waters of politics to establish this. For he
himself has underscored the social connections of his
philosophy and has made abundantly clear at what
points the facts of existing American culture depart
from the promise of American traditions. It may be
that there are many American traditions—the tradition of Hamilton and Jefferson, of Calhoun and Lincoln. But the dominant American traditions are those
which are embodied, even if incompletely, in distinctive
American institutions, and in the ideals, practices, and
manners which led Europeans to make the discovery,
before Americans themselves, that we were a democracy. It is as the philosopher of American democracy
that John Dewey has been able to capture the imagination and allegiance of thousands of people who have
only a dim idea of his technical achievements. What
he has attempted to do is to show how the ideals of
American democracy, born in an agrarian economy,
must be conceived in this era of corporate industry in
order that our liberties be preserved and our security
extended. It is not enough to invoke the principles so
eloquently formulated by Jefferson, whom Dewey regards as the great architect of the American dream.
For their promise can be made good only insofar as a
new set of social relations produce the conditions necessary for their effective fulfillment. Chief among these
conditions are: opportunity for continuous employment, wide social security, democratic participation of
producers and consumers not only in government but
in economic life, an open educational career to all
children, encouragement of complete freedom of scientific inquiry, the pooling of intelligence to plan for a

public welfare upon which can be built independent personal lives.

The great difference between the economy of Jefferson and the economy of present-day America is the result, according to Dewey, of the scientific and technological revolutions of the last hundred and fifty years. The consequences of the application of science to material culture are more manifest in America than anywhere else in the world. In Dewey's philosophy we have a sustained and systematic attempt to take the pattern of scientific inquiry as a model for knowledge and action in all fields. He does not recognize any such thing as "the bankruptcy of science" or even "a crisis of science" except in the technical sense which marks a phase of rapid development. The life of democracy in our day and age depends upon "taking the method of science home into our own controlling attitudes and dispositions, employing the new techniques as means of directing our thoughts and efforts to a planned control of social forces."

Dewey's emphasis upon science corrects, purifies, and raises to the plane of a philosophy of life certain pervasive features of everyday American experience. There is a folk trait, developed in the course of rapid, physical conquest of a virgin continent, which judges proposals, new ideas, and people by fruits, consequences, and works. "The argument from Missouri" is an argument heard from Maine to California. It often takes crude forms in its impatience with abstractions. And like most folk attitudes it has not a highly developed sense of relevance, so that it sometimes looks to the wrong set of consequences to test professions. What is called American practicality is not revealed pre-

eminently in American commercialism. The latter owes
its leading role in world economy more to the natural
wealth of America and the technology-mindedness of
Americans than to its trading genius. Under equal conditions of competition, American business men can
easily be played for "suckers" by their European con-
freres, as they so often are even today. In commerce
as in war, overwhelming strength can triumph without
shrewdness. American practicality is more conspicuously expressed in the tendency to find out "how
things work," in the concern for instruments, methods,
techniques, in a rough and ready inventiveness which
shows remarkable freedom from ritualism or worship
of the past. In Dewey, the positive features of this attitude appear, accompanied by the desire to liberate it
from the habit of taking the nearest, the easiest, the
most superficial consequences as the hallmarks of significant quality. Like William James, Dewey regards
the cult of quantity and the worship of "the bitch-
goddess Success," which are indisputable aspects of
the American culture pattern, as corrupting elements
in American life, not really a form of intelligent practicality, and neither logically nor psychologically integral to the pragmatic temper.

There is another aspect of American faith which reflects itself in Dewey's philosophy. This is the sense,
which underlies American energy and tempo, so much
of it wasteful, that the world is not yet completely
made but in the making. The physical frontier is gone
but the motor dispositions with which it was met are
kept alive by education in school and home, and await
new social frontiers to be released. The great mass of

Americans is not yet ideology ridden. There is a certain distaste for sharp disjunctions of policy, and a popular belief that in times of crisis ways of action can be found which will combine the best aspects of all proposals. This distrust of ideology unfortunately often extends to distrust of theory. No one approves of drifting or muddling through, even when these are in fact the only terms that accurately characterize American national policy. Nonetheless, there is still an optimism about possibilities in America, a willingness to try things out, if they are not labeled by ideologies with frightening connotations, that suggests youthfulness to some, naïveté to others.

For Dewey, too, "the United States are not yet made." He sees its life as a perpetual open frontier. He is always stressing the existence of genuine possibilities. Courage to try them out is high in his scale of virtues. But the mood of optimism is present in a chastened form. The vision of possibilities is sobered by fidelity to a rigorous scientific method which evaluates them in the light of objective conditions. For it is objective conditions that determine the range within which relevant and effective application of ideals can be made. The future is not uniquely determined as it is in a block-universe (strictly speaking there is no genuine future in such a universe); but neither does it permit all degrees of freedom. Any proposal for action which falls outside the range of relevant and effective application is illusory and Utopian. Once again we observe how an indigenous quality of the American culture pattern is not merely expressed in Dewey's thought but criticized and transformed by a typical emphasis. And to criticize or transform, to supplement or strengthen the values embodied in a culture, is just what it means to have a philosophy of culture. If philosophy literally reflected or mirrored social life, as so many social interpretations of philosophy assume, what would be the need of it?

The strength of individualism in American life, not only as a doctrine of self-help, but as a conception of society made up of socially and politically equal individuals, is rooted in pioneer traditions. The complex interrelationships of an industrial age, and the objective insecurities of capitalism in decline, have made the theory of self-help a pathetic anachronism. Even philanthropy has acquired a corporate character. Dewey was the first to speak of "rugged individualism" as "ragged individualism." Yet part of this faith in individualism was an appreciation of the uniqueness, the significance, and the right to be different, of individuals. In no country of the world have origins counted for so little. Nowhere has social mobility been so marked. Individual works, not position in a feudal hierarchy, defined social status. Despite the glaring facts of class division, both the official and popular mythology of America until recently pictured our country as a classless society.

In the writings of Dewey a new conception of individualism is offered in order to preserve the individuality which the old economic individualism has crushed. Its main features have already been described in previous chapters. It makes social control of production central, not private or public relief. We have seen how all of Dewey's theories reinforce the moral that to cherish free individuals and the value of individuality *in abstracto* is not sufficient. Unless plans and programs are devised to produce the social conditions in which free individuals can thrive, talk about individualism, old or new, is an apologetic diversion. Dewey's interest in plans and programs has always carried him much further than the bulk of the American people has been prepared to go. In politics he has invariably taken his place among the progressive *avant-garde*. In recent years his support of a program which demands that the profit system be remade in the interest of "enduring opportunity for productive and creative activity" of free individuals, has brought him to a position which marks the high-water point in the development of an indigenous American radicalism. Some who speak in the name of his philosophy have tried to portray it as the theoretical generating source of the New Deal. Dewey himself, however, has been consistently critical of the contradictions in its domestic policy, the irresponsible character of its foreign policy, and the fundamental objective from which flows its confusion, its wastefulness, and its half-hearted reforms, viz., the preservation of capitalism.

John Dewey is the philosopher of American democracy at a time when the principles of democracy are in retreat in almost all countries and under fire in his own. He firmly believes that America is still a land of promise and opportunity. He holds that a happy conjunction of history, peoples, resources, and seminal ideals makes the vision of freedom and welfare, which led so many to these shores, a live possibility for our own times. The realization of the vision depends in

part upon our faith in it, in part upon our willingness
to risk something in action to vindicate this faith, in
part upon the intelligence we display in the course of
the action.

For whom does John Dewey speak? He himself would
characteristically say he speaks for no one but himself. But ideas cannot become instruments of social
change, or even alter the climate of opinion, unless they
are related to interests and needs. Dewey's ideas have
already won a wide hearing and a not inconsiderable,
but unorganized, following. In whose interests, then,
does he speak? He tells us that "democracy is concerned not with freaks or geniuses or heroes or divine
leaders but with associated individuals in which each by
intercourse with others somehow makes the life of each
more distinctive." As the philosopher of American
democracy, he speaks, then, for those whom we have
previously designated by the phrase "the plain man."
This is still too vague. In America everyone thinks of
himself as "a plain man," and Dewey does not speak for
everyone. But we can list in broad outline the groups
whose interests are represented in Dewey's philosophy.
He speaks first of all for those who do productive labor
of hand or brain, who desires not only continuous work
but significant work commensurate with their capacities.
He speaks for those for whom cultural and intellectual
freedom is the salt and yeast without which the bread
of subsistence is stale and flat. He speaks for those who
wish to see the crucial problems and conflicts of our day
settled by a voluntary consent obtained by persuasion,
and not by terror and bloodshed. He speaks for those
who wish to make our cultural heritage and total social

capital available to every American child. He speaks finally for those who repine not over what America was or might have been but who still have hope for what America may yet be.

BIBLIOGRAPHICAL REFERENCES

A complete bibliography of the writings of John Dewey would fill a fair-sized volume. Three convenient collections of John Dewey's writings, edited by Dr. Joseph Ratner, may be consulted by the interested reader.

The Philosophy of John Dewey, Henry Holt and Co. 1928.
Characters and Events, 2 Vol., Henry Holt and Co. 1929.
Intelligence in the Modern World, Modern Library Giant. 1939.

The following books and articles by John Dewey discuss the questions treated in the various chapters.

Chapter I
Contemporary American Philosophy, Vol. II, edited by Adams and Montague. Macmillan. 1930.

Chapter II
Philosophy and Civilization, Minton, Balch and Company. 1931.
Reconstruction in Philosophy, Henry Holt and Company. 1920.
Article on *Philosophy* in *Encyclopedia of the Social Sciences.*

Chapter III and Chapter IV
Essays in Experimental Logic, University of Chicago Press. 1917.
Experience and Nature, Open Court Publishing Co. 1925 and 1929.

The Quest for Certainty, Minton, Balch and Company. 1929.

How We Think, D. C. Heath & Co. 2nd edition, 1933.

Chapter V
Logic: The Theory of Inquiry, Henry Holt and Company. 1938.

Chapter VI
Human Nature and Conduct, Henry Holt and Company. 1922.

Philosophy and Civilization, supra.

"The Unity of the Human Being," *Intelligence in the Modern World,* ed. by Ratner, *supra.*

Chapter VII
Ethics, Henry Holt and Company, 2nd ed., 1932.

Theory of Valuation, University of Chicago Press. 1939.

Chapter VIII
The Public and Its Problems, Henry Holt and Company. 1927.

Individualism Old and New, Minton, Balch and Company. 1930.

Liberalism and Social Action, Minton, Balch and Company. 1935.

"Authority and Social Change," Harvard Tercentenary Publications.

"Means and Ends," *New International,* 1938.

Chapter IX
Democracy and Education, Macmillan Company. 1916.

Experience and Education, Macmillan Company. 1938.

Chapter X
Art As Experience, Minton, Balch and Company. 1935.

John Dewey

Chapter XI
  A Common Faith, Yale University Press. 1934.
  Experience and Nature, supra.

Chapter XII
  Characters and Events, supra.
  Liberalism and Social Action, supra.